P9-BIY-765

Diva:

BARBRA STREISAND
AND THE MAKING
OF A SUPERSTAR

Edited by
Ethlie Ann Vare

BOULEVARD BOOKS
NEW YORK

DIVA: BARBRA STREISAND AND THE MAKING OF A
SUPERSTAR

A Boulevard book / published by arrangement with
Ethlie Ann Vare

PRINTING HISTORY
Boulevard trade paperback edition / October 1996

The Putnam Berkley World Wide Web site address is
http://www.berkley.com/berkley

ISBN: 1-57297-166-5

BOULEVARD
Boulevard Books are published by The Berkley Publishing Group,
200 Madison Avenue, New York, New York 10016.
BOULEVARD and its logo are trademarks
belonging to Berkley Publishing Corporation.

PRINTED IN THE UNITED STATES OF AMERICA

10 9 8 7 6 5 4 3 2 1

Dedicated to my Dad

CONTENTS

CONTENTS

viii

COPYRIGHT ACKNOWLEDGMENTS

ACKNOWLEDGMENTS

*T*his book was impossible. It was made possible only through the talent, generosity and hard work of a bunch of people. I would like to take a moment to thank them.

Foremost are the writers and critics whose works are collected here— a sampling of the smartest popular journalism written over the past 30 years. I thank the authors, their agents and their lawyers, for allowing me to include them.

A special thank-you to Kimberly Ball, my research assistant, who took a snowstorm of paperwork and made it manageable for a terminally right-brained no-hoper like me. Her soft-spoken gentility belies her intellectual tenacity.

My gratitude to my agent, Madeleine Morel, who is always in my corner. We started working together when a Macintosh was something you ate and Windows were something you looked out of. Typewriters were what you wrote books on.

I remain in awe of my editor, Elizabeth Beier, who champions my projects with an energy and verve that are dizzying. If her enthusiasm were marketable . . . it would probably be illegal.

I want to thank the fans, friends and colleagues of Barbra Streisand, whose ardor, expertise and zeal have added so much to my education.

But mostly, I want to thank Barbra Streisand herself, for being such a fascinating, frustrating and fulfilling subject.

INTRODUCTION

*T*his is not a biography of Barbra Streisand. It is the stuff of biography. Biography in the raw. It's the real deal: pop history as it unfolded. Barbra Streisand as she was perceived—criticized, analyzed, assessed, adored, castigated and venerated—as it happened, when it happened, by the people who were there, watching.

I love television documentaries. And I don't know about you, but what I love most is the film clips. The brief glimpses into that time, that place, as it really looked and sounded and felt. Of less interest to me is the narration, the opinion of the documentary makers. I want to make up my own mind. I want raw footage.

This book is all raw footage. Whatever conclusions I've reached are irrelevant. Draw your own conclusions; this is a do-it-yourself documentary. You probably already have an opinion about Barbra Streisand, anyway, or you wouldn't have picked up the book. And if you don't . . . I guarantee you, you will by the time you've finished reading what some of popular culture's most compelling commentators have said over the past 30 years about one of popular culture's most compelling figures.

There are some amazing voices collected here. Gloria Steinem profiled Barbra Streisand, back when the groundbreaking feminist author was still a freelance journalist, earning a living writing for women's magazines. Alongside her—and I'm sure this is one of the few times they find themselves between the same covers—is Camille Paglia, the controversial postfeminist academic, writing, of all things, a review of Streisand's comeback concert.

Isaac Bashevis Singer—winner of the Nobel Prize, the National Book Award, the Newberry Award, more awards than you can count, for his elegant prose in both English and Yiddish—is represented, debating himself (!) as to whether the movie *Yentl* captured the spirit of his short story.

Also represented is rabbi-turned-novelist Chaim Potok, whose description of his conversations with Streisand is an extraordinary blend of perspicacity and naiveté.

There's a piece by essayist Pete Hamill, the tough kid from Brooklyn who went on to befriend the glitterati . . . and understand them better than any newshound should. There's an amazing series of insights from Broadway impresario Jerome Weidman, who may not have *made* Streisand a star, but certainly held the ladder steady and watched her climb. There's an in-depth analysis of Streisand-as-musical-instrument from the legendary, eccentric and oh-so-brilliant pianist Glenn Gould.

And, of course, there's gossip gossip gossip—from the likes of columnist Rex Reed, novelist Rona Jaffe, and screenwriter Nora Ephron. There's humor (I love how New York Jewish Barbra affected Texas Baptist Andy Tiemann's love life) and memorabilia (Tom Galyean is *the* Streisand collector's expert) and filmographies and discographies and everything else I thought was cool.

That was my job as not-exactly-biographer. I got to find all this stuff, pick out the coolest, and save it for you. Not a bad job, in all. Especially when the cool stuff is about someone like Barbra Streisand.

Barbra Streisand's fingerprints are all over every article in this book. Well, almost: Some journalists—the British, particularly—escaped her fine Italian hand. Fine Brooklyn hand. Her control is so finely tuned that she seems aware of every glance, every word, every picture, every nuance in her career. Nothing would escape her notice, if she had her way. She walks around picking the lint off her life, trimming every last loose thread from her work. Perfectionist? Barbra Streisand is a perfectionist like Candide is an optimist. Like Muhammad Ali is an egotist. Like Jack the Ripper is a misogynist. This is a woman who has turned overachieving into an art form.

How did this creature ever come out of a railroad flat in Brooklyn? What happened at Erasmus High School in 1959 to spawn this divine aberration?

Barbra Streisand is the biggest-selling female artist in music history. She has recorded 48 albums, which have sold 62 million copies in America. Thirty of those albums have gone gold; twenty have gone platinum; seven of them are multiplatinum.

She won a Grammy award for her first album. She won an Emmy award for her first television special. She won an Academy Award for her first movie. She won a New York Drama Critics' Circle award for her first Broadway show . . . and don't you think the Tony Award folk are kicking themselves for not realizing in 1963 that they'd want to be on this list in 1996?

Streisand was the first female composer to win an Oscar for Best Song ("Evergreen") and the first woman to produce, direct, write and star in a movie (*Yentl*). When she *didn't* win an Oscar for Best Director (for *Prince of Tides*), it made news.

She's unabashedly Jewish, unabashedly female and unabashedly liberal in a national climate that isn't particularly friendly to any of the above. My mother always said Barbra was "too delicatessen for me . . ." a line only another Jew could get away with. Streisand's "too," all right. Too strong, too opinionated, too talented, too picky, too damn certain about everything else she does. Love her for it or hate her for it. Personally, I adore her. Not for her music, because I'm a dyed-in-the-denim rock'n'roller. But because she pulled it off. She walked up to every damn door in town with a "no girls allowed" sign hanging on it, and she walked through.

I did a book like this, another biography-in-the-raw, about Frank Sinatra. It was full of people talking about Frank Sinatra, observing Frank Sinatra, giving their well-considered judgments of Frank Sinatra. In fifty years, Frank Sinatra gave maybe two interviews. He never opened his mouth. We collectively invented him. Barbra Streisand, on the other hand, vehemently invented herself. She gives interview after interview (though she claims to abhor them). She insisted on—and got—final cut over Barbara Walters for their televised conversation.

And yet . . . and yet . . . don't you get the sense that somewhere in there is this incredibly wounded little girl? This gawky kid who never grew into her nose (even though they *promised* she'd grow into her nose). "I'm no Suzanne Pleshette," she shrugged, apologizing for her appearance at age 22. And now—at 54 years of age fergawdsakes!—she still isn't sure that the guys like her for her, and not for the big house and the nice car.

But, hey, that's just my opinion. The narration. Please feel free to ignore it. Write your own introduction. Write your own biography. The research is all done. The fun part is up to you . . .

Barbra
the Singer

I REMEMBER BARBRA

Jerome Weidman

Holiday magazine, November 1963

"The trouble with history," Scott Fitzgerald once observed, "is that you never know when you're living in it."

This is true, but I am not altogether sure that it is a bad thing. All during the late war, for example, whenever I found myself in an interesting place where Things Were Happening, I became aware of a petulant inner voice saying to me: "Now, don't just stand there with your mouth open. Make an effort to remember everything you see and hear. This is an important event. This will be a part of history."

I always made the effort, mainly because I am a coward in the presence of inner voices. Oddly enough, however, now that almost two decades have separated me from those Things That Were Happening, it is rarely the events themselves I remember. It is almost always something peripheral, something small that I was not even aware I was observing—something my inner voice would have spurned—that had lodged itself indelibly in my mind.

"Ah, did you once see Shelley plain?" Robert Browning asked. "And did he stop and speak to you? And did you speak to him again?" The answer is yes, except that, in my case, it was not Shelley. It was a girl named Barbra Streisand, and it never occurred to me at the time that the meeting would be the part of that particular day that would become for me a moment of history.

Late in November of 1961, on a gray afternoon made grayer by my mood, I took a taxi from my doctor's office to the St. James Theatre. The doctor had just told me that, in his opinion and the opinion of a surgeon who had examined me the day before, I would be well advised to go into the hospital almost at once for an abdominal operation.

In five weeks, on January 2, 1962, I was scheduled to go into rehearsal with a musical play called *I Can Get It For You Wholesale* that Harold

Rome and I had written from a novel of mine with the same title. My doctor and the surgeon felt it would be dangerous for me, and unfair to my colleagues, to enter this period of strenuous activity without surgical correction of my abdominal condition. No one enjoys being told he must go under the knife, and if you tell it to a man who is, by his own admission, a coward in the presence of inner voices, it should not be too difficult to imagine the mood in which I traveled across town to the St. James, where David Merrick, the producer of our show, had scheduled an audition.

It was not an important audition. Most of the cast had been chosen during the preceding weeks. What remained to be filled were a few minor roles. I could, without compunction or hesitation, have left the choice of actors and actresses for these remaining roles in the extremely able hands of my colleagues. There is something about the theatre, however, that converts you into a busybody. Or perhaps it is people who possess the instincts of the busybody who are attracted to the theatre. I don't know. I do know that it is as impossible to become partially involved with a show as it is to partially fall in love.

From the moment I became involved with my first theatrical venture, I became involved in all its aspects, about many of which I knew as much as Columbus, when he hoisted sail at Cadiz, knew about Chicago. *I Can Get It For You Wholesale* was my third show, and I would just as soon have left the filling of those remaining minor roles in the hands of my colleagues as I would have left in the same hands the correction of my abdominal outline.

My colleagues may have seen only another colleague in a gray mood coming down the aisle of the St. James that afternoon, but I knew better.

In the self-dramatizing inner mirror that is as indispensable to the writer as his pencil and paper, I saw a doomed man forcing himself to the treadmill of his daily task in order to conceal from his colleagues—who might, if they knew the truth, divert their energies from the joint effort—the fact that he had just been sentenced to death.

This may seem an unfortunate mood in which to audition actors and actresses for minor comic roles. As it turned out, it proved to be the ideal mood. For more than two hours I sat in the darkened theatre, beside Mr. Rome, and behind Mr. Merrick's staff, brooding about my fate and my plumbing, listening to that petulant inner voice say, "Pay attention to your every emotion. Note carefully how you feel. It isn't every day a man gets told he is doomed. You may want to use it some day in a story."

I was aware, as I brooded, that things were happening on stage. None of these things was, however, distracting. There is a quality about all auditions, especially for minor roles in a musical show, that is not unlike the making of pancakes: each one is, of course, different from all the others, the way every set of fingerprints is different, and yet they are all very much alike in general condition.

First, of course, there is the blinding glare of the work light overhead. Everybody agrees, during all auditions, that it would improve matters considerably if somebody hung a shade or even pasted a piece of newspaper around that damned naked bulb, but nobody ever does it. Something about union rules, somebody mutters.

Then there is the stage manager who, at periodic intervals, appears from the wings and, into the dark cavern of the orchestra that conceals the author, the director, the producer's staff and a few other legitimate busybodies, calls out, "Miss Mishallevev Neurokumquat." Or, if he is introducing a male actor, he says, "Mr. Mishallevev Neurokumquat." The names of all unknown actors and actresses, when heard for the first time in a darkened theatre at an audition, sound like an anagram composed of letters taken from the sides of two or more Lithuanian Pullman cars.

If one of the busybodies happens to know the performer, or vice-versa—which is the case quite often, since people in quest of jobs in the theatre go from audition to audition the way Fuller Brush salesmen go from door to door—there is a good deal of delighted squealing, hysterical hand waving, and dubious punning, during which it turns out, always to the surprise to at least *this* busybody, that "Mishallevev Neurokumquat" is actually "Vicky Smith" or "Nicky Jones."

The director asks Vicky or Nicky or, more often, Mishallevev what he or she is going to sing for us. He or she tells us. There is a small fuss about the music. The size of the fuss depends upon whether the performer has brought an accompanist, or is going to use the all-purpose accompanist provided by the producer. The fuss ends. The performer sings. The performer stops singing. From the depths of the darkened auditorium the director says, "Do you have a ballad, Miss Neurokumquat?" Or Vicky. Or Nicky. She or he has.

5

Same fuss with the music. Performer sings ballad. If the performer shows any promise at all, the heads of the busybodies come together like the petals of a flower closing for the night, and a good deal of unintelligible murmuring rises into the shadows. This phase always ends with the director turning back to the stage and asking, "Do you dance?"

If the performer does dance, meaning if she is a professional dancer, she says so, then announces with whom she has studied and in what shows she has danced. If the performer does not dance, meaning she is not a professional dancer and has no talent in that direction, she always says, "Well, I'm not *primarily* a dancer, but I *can* move."

The director says, "Thank you very much." The performer smiles, says "Thank *you* very much," gathers her music, and goes off to the next audition down the street. The busybodies in the darkened theatre shift their buttocks, light fresh cigarettes, and the stage manager appears from the wings. "Miss Mishallevev Neurokumquat," he says into the darkened theatre.

When he said, it, on that gray November day, for perhaps the fifteenth or twentieth time, I was trying to remember when I had made my will, and wondering if it would be necessary, before I went into the hospital, to see my lawyer about adding any codicils. The stage manager's numbing syllables had scarcely died away, when I became aware that something unusual was happening on stage. Out of the wings, moving slowly past the stage manager, came not a performer but a fur coat.

This is not, of course, a complete description. To describe what was oozing out onto the stage of the St. James at that moment as a fur coat is about as accurate as describing the North Pole as cool. Still, in times of stress, one clutches at straws. Holding onto that particular straw with desperation, my mind began to paw about for clarifying detail.

First, I grasped the color. The coat was a combination of tans, browns, yellows and whites, all swirling about in great shapeless splotches, like a child's painting of the hide of a piebald pony. Wondering if what I was watching was indeed the hide of a horse, my mind made its next discovery: shape. The flat surface that served as the body of the coat was adorned at the neck, the cuffs, and the hem by great fat rolls of not quite but almost jet-black foam rubber that looked like flexible sections of sewer pipe. Wondering desperately where I had seen this coat before, and knowing damned well it had not been on any human being who had ever walked a city street or a country lane in my presence, my mind finally disgorged the startling but satisfying answer: this was the coat worn by Michael Strogoff, The Courier Of The Czar, in the movie of the same name to which Miss Tischler had taken our 4B class as a Washington's Birthday treat when I was a boy of nine in P.S. 188.

With this much settled, my mind was free to record several other interesting details. Out of the bottom of the coat, helping—but only barely helping—to support it, protruded a couple of very shapely legs that ended in a couple of very dirty tennis sneakers. Out of the top of the coat stuck a ball of brownish steel wool, the kind one uses to scrub pots and pans, that might have been hair. Somewhere around the middle of the coat, where Michael Strogoff had belted his sword, something—I could see no sign of a hand—was supporting a bright red plastic briefcase.

And, oh yes, the entire contraption was being tugged forward across the stage by a short leash which, on closer examination, proved to be a long nose.

The coat moved forward perhaps five feet. The red briefcase fell to the stage with a loud slap. The coat collapsed into an enveloping puddle concealing the briefcase, then rose slowly. For a moment the briefcase hung in the air, like a cotton ball caught in the spray of a bubbling fountain, then shot out in an arc, like an orange pip squeezed between thumb and forefinger. The fur coat changed shape. It hurtled up and out like a football player leaving the ground in a flying tackle, and caught the briefcase before it bounced. But then the *coat* bounced. It hit the stage, crumpled into a wad, then rose straight up into the air, all its rolls of black foam rubber billowing wildly, and from the bottom of the coat the pretty, sneaker-shod legs kicked and clawed, as though trying to get back to earth. They did, with a thump that sent the red briefcase out in another flying arc. It landed on top of the piano, burst open like a melon hitting a sidewalk, slid across the shiny wood, and showered a mass of sheet music into the startled face of the accompanist. The leash pulled the fur coat around to face the darkened theatre. Out of the wad of tangled steel wool came a twanging voice dripping with the ambiance of Bushwick Avenue.

"That guy is a liar," the voice said, and the coat jerked in the direction of the vanished stage manager. "My name is not Mishallevev Neurokum-

7

quat. It's Barbra Streisand. With only two 'a's. In the name, I mean. I figure that third 'a' in the middle, who needs it? What would you like me to do?"

Nobody answered. For a moment I did not understand why. Then I looked at Mr. Rome and my other colleagues. Tears were streaming from their eyes. From their mouths emerged meaningless whimpers. Their hands were clutching their navels. They were helpless with laughter. As for me, I did not realize until much later that, in the struggle to catch my own breath, I had, for the first time since I had left my doctor's office, completely forgotten that I was a doomed man.

The nose came forward, dragging from the depths of the foam rubber collar a face. It squinted down into the darkness with monumental distaste.

"What are y'awl? Dead or somethin'?" Miss Streisand demanded. "I said what would you like me to do?"

"Can you sing?" the director asked.

"Can I sing?" Miss Streisand said to the work light. The squint swung down toward us again, like a whip. "If I couldn't sing, would I have the nerve to come out here in a thing like this coat?"

"Okay," the director said. "Sing."

"Sing!" Miss Streisand said to the work light, and I wondered if all her friendships with inanimate objects took shape as quickly as this, or whether this particular work light was one with which rapport had been established long ago. "Even a jukebox you don't just say sing, you gotta first punch a button with the name of a song on it," Miss Streisand said irritably into the darkened theatre. "What should I sing?"

"Anything you want," the director said.

The squint gave place to a look of wide-eyed, childish astonishment, and it occurred to me that Miss Streisand was as pretty as her legs.

"Anything?" she said incredulously.

"Anything," the director said.

Miss Streisand turned to the accompanist and said, "Play that thing it's on top."

What proved to be on top may not actually be the funniest song ever written, but it certainly came out that way when filtered through Miss Streisand's squint, fur coat, gestures and vocal cords. It was what, as a veteran of many auditions, I have come to identify as a "Why?" song. Just as some novelists, trapped by the problem of exposition, frequently solve it by causing one character to feed leading questions to another, so some lyricists, facing the problem of how—in a medium that has already said it thousands of times—to say "I love you" in a new way, solve it by asking a rhetorical question, then go on to answer it. "Why am I so happy?" Because, stupid, I love you. "Why does the sky seem brighter today than usual?" Because, you idiot, today I met you.

Miss Streisand's song, traditionally enough, asked why she loved a boy named, if memory serves, Arnie Fleisher. The answer, however, was not traditional, because Miss Streisand, in the midst of making it, remembered that she also loved *another* boy. I do not know his name. Not because memory, usually so dependable, is not serving in this instance. The truth is I never heard that second boy's name. The words were engulfed in the laughter of the theatre professionals around me. When Miss Streisand had finished, and the theatre walls had settled back into place, the director was just able to honor the tradition of his trade: "Do you have a ballad?" he managed to gasp.

Miss Streisand looked at him as though she were in Aix, where she had been pacing about worriedly for days, and he were the boy who had just arrived with news from Ghent.

"Ooh, have I got a ballad!" she squealed. "Wait till you *hear*!"

She made a complicated flopping gesture in the direction of the accompanist, revealing for the first time a pair of slender, beautiful hands only partially disfigured by the sort of blood-red talons once popular with the artists who used to illustrate Sax Rohmer's stories about Fu Manchu. The accompanist, who was by now clearly under her spell, seemed to know exactly what Miss Streisand meant. From the tangled mess that had spilled out of the red briefcase, he plucked a sheet of music and struck a few chords.

Miss Streisand folded those lovely hands in front of that appalling coat, looked up toward the second balcony, opened her mouth, and an extraordinary thing happened.

Softly, in a voice as true as a plumb line and pure as the soap that floats, with the quiet authority of someone who had seen the inevitable, as simply and directly and movingly as Homer telling about the death of Hector, she told the haunting story of a girl who had stayed "too long at the fair."

It was a song, of course, and a good one. But emerging through the voice and personality of this strange child, it became more than that. We were hearing music and words, but we were experiencing what one gets only from great art: a moment of revealed truth. This, you suddenly felt, is the way it is. This, you finally understood, was what T. S. Eliot had meant when he wrote that the world ends "not with a bang but a whimper." And this, you grasped as you wiped away your tears, was what people meant when they spoke of the X quality that makes a star.

Miss Streisand got the job, and I went to the hospital. There, after I came out of the anaesthetic and discovered that my death sentence had been, in Mark Twain's phrase, greatly exaggerated, I was visited by my collaborator. Mr. Rome is a man of many talents. Not the least of these is an extraordinary capacity for friendship. He brought with him a bottle of whisky and news of our project. After we had made a small inroad on the former, he started on the latter.

"I've been thinking of this Streisand kid," Mr. Rome said.

"So have I," I said.

It turned out that our thoughts were not too far apart. Miss Streisand had been hired to play the role of a garment center secretary called Miss Marmelstein.

As conceived originally, in the novel I published in 1937 and in the play Mr. Rome and I wrote in 1961, the role of Miss Marmelstein is not exactly the focal point of the enterprise, and yet you've really got to have her.

The hero of *I Can Get It For You Wholesale* moves up in the world and, from doing business on the pavements, he begins to function in an office. To satisfy the most minimal demands of verisimilitude, any representation of an office must have a desk and a secretary. Mr. Rome and I had spent very little time writing in the desk, and not much more establishing the secretary. In our original script she was, like the desk, just another piece of furniture.

Until Miss Streisand, aged nineteen, came along.

"You let a kid like that come out on a stage," said Mr. Rome, who hates to be called a Veteran Showman, perhaps because he happens to be a Veteran Showman, "and things are going to happen. You keep her just a piece of furniture, saying things like *Call for you, Mr. Jones* or *Here's those papers you asked for, Mr. Smith*, and the audience is going to forget all about Mr. Jones and why he's getting that call, or Mr. Smith and why he asked for those papers. They're going to be watching that girl. Watching her and expecting her to do something. Unless we give her something to do—and it can't be something extraneous, it's got to be part of the story—unless we do that, the story is going to go out the window."

It didn't. Because Mr. Rome was right, of course, and we set about at once, using my incision as a temporary desk, giving Miss Streisand plenty to do. The way she did it is, as Frank Sullivan's cliché expert might put it, a matter of history: she stopped the show on opening night and every night thereafter.

Between those happy occasions and my first glimpse of Barbra at the St. James audition, our paths crossed frequently, about as frequently as the paths of a pair of Siamese twins set afloat in a sealed barrel on a turbulent river.

Out of the eleven and a half weeks between the start of rehearsals and the New York opening at the Shubert Theatre on March 23, 1962—a period that made, for at least one participant, the Battle of Cannae look like a quiet hour with Queen Victoria's *Leaves From the Journal of Our Life in the Highlands*—a number of moments with Miss Streisand loom up out of the haze of battle, moments that bring into sharper focus that first generalized impression and help to convert, at least for the author of these notes, a talent into a human being.

The first moment came, appropriately enough, on the first day of rehearsals. In a ritual as fixed by tradition as the moves in a minuet, the day started with the "first reading by the cast." Sitting in a half-circle on stage, the actors and actresses read the play to the authors and the director. It is always a time of curious intimacy. Everybody has the same feeling: *please God, make it a hit!* Other emotions will succeed this one, many of them revoltingly more intimate. But none will ever recapture that early fragment of shared innocence. It occurred to me, as I listened and watched, that the only person who was not sharing it with me was Miss Streisand.

As the others read their parts, as the director and Mr. Rome and I

11

listened, I became aware that Miss Streisand was doing more than making the occasional note next to a line with which many actors and actresses punctuate the reading. Miss Streisand, scribbling busily, might have been racing the clock to get her translation of the *Decline And Fall* to the printer before other activities, such as rehearsing a musical play, claimed her attention.

When the reading ended, I watched her go up to the press agent and engage him in a long, animated conversation. It seemed to deal with Miss Streisand's composition, a good deal of which, to judge by the expression on the press agent's face, he found perplexing. I wandered across to them and, now a full-fledged busybody, asked what was happening.

"Get a load of this," the press agent said. "I asked the cast to give me some stuff for the biographical notes in the program. Look what this dame gives me."

He thrust Miss Streisand's composition at me. I read: "Not a member of the Actor's Studio, Miss Streisand is nineteen and this is her first Broadway show. Born in Madagascar and reared in Rangoon, she attended Erasmus Hall High School in Brooklyn. She appeared off-Broadway in a one-nighter entitled *Another Evening With Harry Stoones*. She has appeared at New York's two best known supper clubs, the Bon Soir and the Blue Angel, and was on Mike Wallace's PM East eight times, the Jack Paar show twice, the Gary Moore show, the Tonight show with Groucho Marx, and is being sought for many top TV entertainments this season."

I looked up and said, "Was it hot in Madagascar?"

"How the hell should I know?" said Miss Streisand. "I never been to the damn place."

"That's my point," the press agent said. "It's a phony. Nobody reading that will believe you."

"What the hell do I care?" said Miss Streisand. "It's me I'm worrying about, not anybody reads the program. I'm so sick and tired of being born in Brooklyn, I could plotz. Whad I do? Sign a contract I gotta be born in Brooklyn? Who asked for it?"

"Don't you like Brooklyn?" I said.

"What's that got to do with it?" she demanded. "I hapna *love* Brooklyn, but it's like the name Barbara. Every day with the third 'a' in the middle, you could go out of your mind. I mean, what are we here for?

Every day the same thing? No change? No variety? Why get born? Every day the same thing, you might as well be dead. I've had nineteen years Barbara with three 'a's' and all my life born in Brooklyn. Enough is enough. Don't you understand that?"

I certainly did. I had been nineteen myself once.

"Where did you study singing?" asked Mr. Rome, who had joined us.

"Who had time to study singing?" she said. "Nineteen years, and I haven't even had time to get out of *Brooklyn* yet!"

Her conception of time was clarified for me a week later during a ten-minute rehearsal break. I spent five of those minutes discussing something with Mr. Rome, then went out into the lobby to make a phone call. There were two booths. Both were occupied and both had several people waiting in front of their doors. When the stage manager's whistle sounded the end of the ten-minute break, everybody in the lobby hurried back to the rehearsal. Everybody except me and, I discovered as the lobby emptied, Miss Streisand.

She hurried into one booth. I went into the other. It crossed my mind, as I dropped my dime into the slot, that while I would not be holding up anybody by returning late to the rehearsal, since I was not needed on stage, Miss Streisand was very much needed and would be holding up everybody. The truth of what had crossed my mind was confirmed a moment later.

"Barbra!" the voice of the stage manager came bellowing into the lobby. "For God's sake, on stage!"

Imperturbably, from the adjoining booth, Miss Streisand called, "Just one second! Be right there!" I thought the next sound I would hear would be the opening of the door of the adjoining phone booth, followed by Miss Streisand's footsteps hurrying back to her rehearsal. I was wrong. The next sound I heard was the ping of a coin dropping into the slot in the next phone booth, followed by Miss Streisand's voice saying, "Operator, get me Los Angeles, huh?"

What she got, in addition to Los Angeles, was a bawling out from the director that, even though I thought it completely justified, disturbed me. She took it head down, face concealed by a curtain of tumbled hair, while her hands made small twitching motions in her lap. After all, I thought miserably, she's only a kid. A couple of weeks later, the morning after the Philadelphia opening, I discovered that to describe Miss Streisand—who

13

was clearly a genius, and even more clearly destined for the heights—as "only a kid" was not unlike identifying Savonarola as "only an investigator."

It had been a rough opening, and the reviews, which were not exactly uniform, reminded one of Mr. George Kaufman's definitions of the word "mixed" in the phrase "mixed reviews": "good and lousy." The director had assembled the cast at the back of the theatre for one of those sessions known as "notes."

In the theatre this always means the same thing: the cast gathered in an uneasy cluster, sitting cheek by jowl as though to share their bodily warmth against the winds of a cold world; listening, in a manner that can only be described as "nervously scared sincere," to the notes the director has made on their last performance.

I had been on the phone with my agent in New York, assuring him that out-of-town critics had a tendency to overuse the word "disaster," and so I arrived at this particular "notes" session a few minutes late.

I do not know, therefore, if Miss Streisand had done anything special on this particular occasion to annoy the director, or whether the cold rage with which he was addressing her was due to nothing more than the tension under which we were all living plus our heroine's by now established talent for sabotaging any executive attempt at organization.

As the director's words went hurtling toward her like so many venom-tipped darts, the rest of the cast seemed to cringe away, as though afraid to be splashed by criticism so savage and so total that it might be permanently disfiguring even to those who happened to be in the neighborhood. My heart, which should have been sticking around to take care of its owner's bruises, insisted on going out to Miss Streisand.

There she sat, again head down, her face again concealed by that curtain of tumbled hair, her hands again making those small twitching motions in her lap. I was so upset by what was happening to this helpless sliver of a girl under the lashing of the director's verbal knout—after all, she was just a kid, wasn't she—that I almost committed what is in the theatre the equivalent of, at a royal level, turning one's back on the sovereign, namely, interfering in public with the director's total authority over the cast. I was saved from this sin not only by the fact that this was, after all, my third show and, as Mr. Phil Silvers once put it: "If you hang around, you learn!," but also, and in the main, because the sight of Miss Streisand's suffering filled me with so much pity and horror that I could neither speak nor move.

When the holocaust was over, I managed to pull myself together sufficiently to approach the stricken child. She was still sitting there, all alone now, the others having fled as though from a carrier of the plague, her head still bowed, her face still hidden by the curtain of hair, her hands still twitching spasmodically in her lap.

"Barbra," I mumbled, my voice shaking, "I'm sorry, kid."

Her head came up. The curtain of hair fell back, revealing not the tears I expected, but a puzzled frown that took me by surprise.

"Listen, Jerry," she said, and she lifted from her lap not only what her twitching hands had been doing while my heart had been bleeding for her, but also the pencil with which she had done it: the floor plan of a one-room apartment criss-crossed with innumerable sketches of furniture arrangements. She said, "I got this new apartment on Forty-fourth Street, and it's real nice, you know, but the damn fireplace, it's all the way over here on *this* wall, so where the hell would *you* put the studio couch, huh?"

I cannot remember if I told her. I would like to think, now that the campaign is over, that I did. After all, it is not often that one can truly say yes, one did see Shelley plain. And about almost nobody I have ever met— nobody, that is, I have ever met who is nineteen—do I feel I can say with confidence: Barbra Streisand, like Shelley, is going into the record books.

Not only because she has genius, which I discovered on that first day at the audition in the St. James Theatre; nor even because she is what the lawyers call *sui generis*, or unique, which is what every star must be.

Barbra Streisand is going into the books, near the top of whatever list gets compiled, because she possesses one other ingredient necessary to stardom, and I discovered it on that dismal morning in Philadelphia: she is made of copper tubing.

15

*A*ccording to *Playbill*, Barbra Streisand, who is the harassed secretary, Miss Marmelstein, in "I Can Get It For You Wholesale," and sings a self-exposing, show-stopping song called "Miss Marmelstein," was born in Madagascar, reared in Rangoon, and educated at Erasmus Hall High School, in Brooklyn. We asked her about her birthplace in the course of a post-matinée chat we had with her at Sardi's last week.

"What does it matter where you are born?" she said. "Do you think it would be all right for me to wear a long wool dress to a birthday party that the Lichee Tree Restaurant, in Greenwich Village, is giving for me tomorrow night? I got it in Filene's Basement, in Boston, for a hundred dollars reduced to twenty-five. I buy most of my clothes in thrift shops. Department stores are too expensive, and the salespeople there are so mean! They're a haughty bunch of people. In thrift shops, they're not mean. My birthday was really a couple of weeks ago; I'm twenty. The owners of the Lichee Tree are old friends of mine. I grew up with Chinese people. I used to babysit for a Chinese couple in Brooklyn; they had a restaurant and taught me to enjoy Chinese dishes. I often go to Chinatown to eat late at night. You get wonderful white hot breads with the center filled with shrimp at the little coffee shops there. Only ten cents! I love food. I look forward to it all day. My body responds to it. Everything else seems so nebulous. I love broiled mushrooms and watercress. I began to sing in nightclubs when I was eighteen—I was at the Bon Soir and the Blue Angel, and on Tuesday, May 22nd, I'm going back to the Bon Soir for two weeks—and when people offered to buy me a drink I'd ask for potatoes. I never *saw* a nightclub until I performed in one. The Bon Soir hired me after I'd had a week's engagement in a restaurant in the Village, and I got *that* engagement by winning a talent contest for singing. I was given a sort of good voice. I never was in Manhattan until I was fourteen.

I came over to see 'The Diary of Anne Frank.' My father, who was a Ph.D. and taught English literature and psychology in high schools, died when I was fifteen months old, and my mother never liked to leave Brooklyn. She's there now. She did come to the opening night of 'Wholesale,' but I don't think she understood what I was trying to do in it. Why should she? The things that interest her about me are whether I'm eating enough and whether I am warmly enough dressed. She's a very simple, nonintellectual, nontheatrical person who lives and breathes."

Miss Streisand, who in her secretarial role drew such (nonpejorative) adjectives as "oafish," "brash," "plain," and "homely" from the critics, is in private life an animated, poised, and unconventionally beautiful young woman, with an aquiline nose, great big soulful eyes, and great big soulful eyelashes. During our talk, she consumed, soulfully, three buttered rolls, a clam juice, a V-8, a crabmeat with asparagus, and a 7-Up.

"The best fried chicken I know of comes with a TV dinner," she said. "I have a railroad flat in the East Sixties, but it's getting too small. It's getting too small because I just bought two marvelous Victorian cabinets with glass shelves. I got them in a shop at Eighty-third Street and Columbus Avenue, called Foyniture Limited. That's how it's spelled. I like to get shawls that I can wear instead of a coat, and that can also serve as bedcovers. I was bald until I was two. I think I'm some sort of Martian. I exist on my will power, being Taurus. My birthday was April 24th. I hate the name Barbara; I dropped the second 'a,' and I think I'll gradually cut the whole thing down to B. That will save exertion in handwriting. I sometimes call myself Angelina Scarangella, which won't. I used to study acting with three different people, and I didn't want any of them to know I was studying with the others, so I took the name Angelina Scarangella part of the time to throw them off the track. I had it printed on match covers. Allan Miller, on West Forty-eighth Street, was my first teacher. He's marvelous. While I was going to him I worked as a clerk in a printing company downtown. Those terrible train rides commuting from Brooklyn! I've never been to the Statue of Liberty or to the top of the Empire State Building. I'd love to visit the Statue of Liberty, because I like water. I suppose I'm going to be famous."

We asked whether she wasn't busy enough without returning to the Bon Soir.

17

"I'm doing it because I can sing the way I want to sing there," she said. "I can't do that in the show. I see the part differently now from the way it was written and directed, and I'd like to do it differently, but I can't. It's difficult for me to find songs that I like, I don't like mooshy love songs. 'Sleepin' Bee,' by Harold Arlen, is my favorite. It's about love, in its way. When I get really rich, I'll have tutors come to my house and teach me languages—including Greek and Japanese. I like Greek and Japanese poetry, but poems can't be translated satisfactorily. I'm reading 'The Conformist,' by Moravia, and some old book by Arnold Bennett that has an *art-nouveau* cover. It's magnificent. I hate diamonds. I like garnets, jade, carnelian, and emeralds, and rubies in old settings. I like interviews—they're still a novelty—but by the time they appear they look funny to me, because my attitude changes from week to week."

"Your attitude toward what?" we asked.

"Oh, toward smoked foods, say," she replied, and we rushed to the phone to file our copy.

"She was an ugly kid with a terrific voice. The first picture I ever took of her is when she's coming from Erasmus High School, to go to work in *Wholesale*. School books in her arms, her hair is stringy and long and falling all into her face. She was a real unattractive girl. I never thought she'd be a movie star; I only thought she had an incredible voice. Even when she did *Funny Girl*, she wasn't pretty. But she was unique."

—photographer BOB DEUTSCH

19

I WAS AN UGLY DUCKLING
Barbra Streisand
Coronet magazine, March 1964

as told to Dixie Dean Harris

I guess in many respects my life parallels Hans Christian Andersen's tale "The Ugly Duckling." Like the duckling, I was teased because I was "different." I was a loner—not *lonely*, understand, but just alone. I wasn't like all the others, and I suppose it bothered me a bit then. But now I wonder if being a little different didn't really help me.

In an age and an art that worships beauty, I'm managing pretty well so far in show business. I got the lead in "Funny Girl," the musical based on the life of Fanny Brice. I've got two record albums that I'm very pleased to see near the top of the weekly show biz polls of best sellers. When it was announced last summer that I would do a concert in San Francisco, the entire house sold out—before a date had been set! And when I sang my "Miss Marmelstein" number in Broadway's "I Can Get It for You Wholesale," it was called a show-stopper.

What really surprises some people—me, too, sometimes—is that I managed to get into show business at all. I knew a casting director during my pre-Broadway days who tried to interest a few agents in me. But after I'd go around to see them, they'd all say the same thing to him: "That funny girl, are you out of your mind?"

So I'm no Suzanne Pleshette. I've got pretty eyes, though, and long lashes. But who notices, with my nose? Jerome Weidman, the author of "Wholesale," described the first time he saw me—or some of me. He told me that when I walked on-stage to audition all he could see was an enormous fur coat, a pair of shapely legs in very dirty tennis sneakers and a pile of brillo-like hair. He said the entire contraption was being tugged forward across the stage by a short leash, which on closer inspection proved to be my nose.

But I haven't worried too much about my nose since the opening of "Wholesale." I really had a good case of first-night jitters. I was so nervous I asked one of the show's backers if he thought I should do something about my nose. "If you do," he answered, "you won't be Barbra Streisand anymore."

That clinched it: No nose job. Because most of all I want to be true to myself. Really, people should be left to be themselves, instead of everyone trying to change everyone else. For what?

For instance, I remember the sneers when I wore long black stockings before they became fashionable all over the country. That still burns me. So if I wore black tights it was to keep warm. I didn't wear them to look bohemian. I never stayed in Greenwich Village. Never hung out in coffee shops. Ridiculous—people sitting around, doing nothing. I never had any friends there. I stayed home and read.

Maybe I do look a little odd sometimes, because I wear bulky fur coats, enormous boots and floppy hats. But New York winters drive me to any and all extremes in trying to keep warm. I hate cold weather.

Some people think my taste in clothes is eccentric. I really don't know why they laugh at my clothes. They're right out of the pages of top fashion magazines. True, some of the magazines date back 30 or 40 years. But I love clothes from the late '20s and '30s. I'm crazy about those old velvets and beaded shoes and long feather boas.

I like thrift shops. I have the greatest collection of old clothes. I paid from $3.50 to $7.50 for them. I once found a Fabiani in one shop. It doesn't matter to me that somebody else wore them first.

And there's another reason why I shop in thrift stores, even though I can afford department stores now. The salespeople in department stores are so mean, a haughty bunch. In thrift shops, nobody's mean.

If that makes me sound like a worried kid from Brooklyn, well, that's what I was for my first 19 years. I was born in the Williamsburg section of Brooklyn on April 24, 1942. (That's Taurus, by the way, and Taurus people exist on their will power.) My father was an English and psychology teacher. He died when I was 15 months old, and my mother remarried when I was 8.

I was one homely kid—the kind that looks absolutely ridiculous with a ribbon in her hair. I yearned for glamour then, and I'd go look for it in the movies. My mother used to hate it when I went to the movies, because I was grouchy for days after. But after seeing all the beautiful things in movies, coming back to where we lived used to depress me. We weren't *poor* poor, but we didn't have anything. Not even a Victrola.

I never got into Manhattan even until I was 14, when I saw my first Broadway play. It was "The Diary of Anne Frank." But I was sitting way up in the balcony. I was very disappointed. It was a sad play and the setting was so dreary. It was drab compared to the movies.

I've always tried to avoid what was drab or ordinary—I mean things like being born in Brooklyn can get to seem so commonplace. I really love Brooklyn, but I played a good trick once on theatergoers and the editors of *Playbill.* Very straight-faced, I said I was born in Madagascar, reared in Rangoon and educated at Erasmus High. My press agent said nobody would believe such a phony line, but I said so what? I told him I'm sick and tired of being born in Brooklyn. I had the same kind of problem with my name. Every day, listening to that 'a' in the middle of Barbara, who needs it? Two 'a's are plenty. For 19 years I had three 'a's and enough is enough. Now I'm Barbra.

After I graduated from Erasmus High School—with a 93 average and a Spanish medal—I moved into Manhattan. I got a job as a clerk and I started taking drama lessons. For a while I was going to three different coaches at once.

I didn't want any of them to know I was studying with the others, so I took the name Angelina Scarangella part of the time to throw them off the track. I had it printed on match covers.

My first break sounds like something out of a movie plot. I was flat broke and I entered a singing contest in a Greenwich Village bar. And I won. A few weeks later I was singing for $108 in a little Village nightclub called the Bon Soir. That led to television appearances. On one, I confounded Mike Wallace by launching into a tirade against milk. My really first appearance on a New York stage was in an off-Broadway revue called "An Evening With Harry Stoones." It was October 21, 1961. I had two songs to sing, a blues one and a comic thing. And that show was well named—it turned out to be just an evening. It opened and closed the same night. And then came my big break in "I Can Get It For You Wholesale."

As Miss Marmelstein, I sang about the trials of an unloved and un-

23

noticed secretary—but in reality I felt far from unloved and/or unnoticed. For one thing, both the critics and the audience showed their approval. And so did Elliot Gould, the play's leading man.

Elliot is a lovely human being, very compassionate and sweet. He's been in show business since he was a kid. He's big, tall and handsome—six three and 190 pounds. And now he's my husband. It's funny, in the play I was the homely secretary and in real life the sort of left-out duckling. But meeting Elliot is like a happy ending. We found each other in "Wholesale." Sure, for me the play was a high spot in my career, but meeting Elliot was a lot more important to me. Here I was, a girl from Brooklyn who never had guys chasing me, never went steady, and a loner. And then the handsome leading man falls in love with me and marries me! It's terrific! Actually my marriage is a very personal thing to me. Although we're very much in show biz, our marriage I'd like to think of as a private thing.

Now we live on Central Park West in a large penthouse duplex that once belonged to Lorenz Hart. We don't have much furniture yet, but so far we've bought an Elizabeth four-poster, a dentist's cabinet—we use it for gloves—some spool cabinets, a theater exit sign and some odds and ends. It has an elegant stairway, so I can make an entrance, and a 55-foot terrace that's larger than the living room.

When I'm not working, I like to sleep, read and eat. I could sleep 15 hours, but usually sleep nine. Eight is okay, but anything less than that makes me grouchy. Food is important, too. I even think of success in terms of food. Success is like having a baked potato come out of the oven just right. Not raw and not overdone. Or, perhaps, a full Chinese meal. I'm devoted to complicated Chinese dishes. Maybe it's because I grew up on hearty but pretty dull European-style cooking.

I used to baby-sit for a Chinese couple in Brooklyn when I was a kid. They had a restaurant and they taught me to enjoy Chinese dishes. I often go to Chinatown late at night to eat. You can get wonderful white hot breads filled with shrimp at the little coffee shops there.

But really, success is more than having perfectly cooked baked potatoes. It's having a $12,000 fur coat instead of a $15 hand-me-down from a thrift shop. It's getting a $15,000 weekly night club salary instead of $108 a week. It's being accepted for what I am, kooky clothes and all, and it's having top American fashion designers like Norman Norell and Bill Blass make a fuss over me.

I have an *awful* stomach that pops in and out and I like to be comfortable when I sing. That's why I wear a lot of Empire dresses. You don't have to wear all those underthings to hold you in. Bill Blass loves my stomach. He said he'd like to design some clothes around it.

And success is being listed in the Encyclopedia Brittanica Yearbook, and having all kinds of admirers. Hollywood's Sidney Skolsky writes about me in his daily column. Johnny Mercer, Harold Arien and George Abbot tell me they're devoted. Writer Robert Ruark called me "the hottest thing to hit entertainment fields since Lena Horne erupted."

But the most important thing that ever happened to me was meeting President Kennedy. The late President invited me to sing at the White House and he stopped to chat after the show. He actually asked me to autograph his album. I told him I wanted a souvenir, too, either the Rose Room or his autograph. I got his autograph.

My singing style and voice have been compared to just about every top female singer. One TV critic went so far as to call me the "American Piaf." Yet I don't think of myself as being a singer, but rather an actress who sings. There's a world of difference. I approach a song as an actress approaches a part. I try to move people when I sing. I try to make little pictures for them which they can feel and visualize. There's no trick in getting up in front of an audience and closing your eyes and singing. That's easy. But to get up there and keep your eyes open and look at your audience and make them feel what you want them to feel—well, that's hard.

Besides acting out my songs, I'm blessed with a big voice. I can skip from whimsies like "Who's Afraid of the Big Bad Wolf" to a serious rendition of "Happy Days Are Here Again." That arrangement, incidentally, came about accidentally when I was practicing it for a TV show. The conductor had me "take it slow" a few times to get the feel of the song. And something happened. I really felt that song. It's a lament for all the tired, disillusioned, hopeful people in the world.

You know, maybe not being a beauty explains my success. Maybe being the girl that guys never looked at twice, and when I sing about that—about being like an invisible woman—people feel like protecting me.

25

When I was on tour, I noticed the audience reaction in a dozen different cities. It was always the same. When I came on stage, people laughed. But when I begin to sing, the audience changes somehow. They're with me. It's as if they'd like to say they're sorry they laughed at me.

I guess it would be easier to describe what I feel about my looks and my career if I used somebody else's words. One evening, New York reporter Jimmy Breslin dropped in on an early rehearsal of "Funny Girl." The stage was bare. Old wooden chairs were the only props. The cast and stagehands were dressed in ordinary work clothes. Breslin later wrote: "Then this girl's voice began to come off this bare stage and it started to reach around the empty theater. Then there was this sort of growl in Barbra Streisand's voice and now you didn't notice the bare stage or the chairs or the guy carrying the ladder. It didn't matter where you were. She is that kind of singer."

When a performer gets that kind of reaction she knows that every bit of hard work was worth it. And I'm ready and willing to keep right on working hard. I want a big career. I want lots of money. I want Broadway—and all the etceteras that go with it.

When I'm good, when I'm pleased with my performance, I feel powerful. I forget about being an ugly duckling. I feel—well, why not—I feel like a swan. Maybe that's it—Brooklyn's ugly duckling and Broadway's beautiful swan.

BEA, BILLIE, AND BARBRA
Newsweek, June 3, 1963

*B*arbra Streisand, a Brooklyn girl with small, sad eyes and an absurd nose, has, for a singer of 20, an absurdly gaudy following. Johnny Mercer, Harold Arlen and George Abbot love her. Robert Roark calls her "the hottest thing to hit the entertainment field since Lena Horne erupted." Her only Broadway show was last year's *I Can Get It For You Wholesale*, and she showed up late 36 times. But its producer, David Merrick, still adores her; he wants her to play Fanny Brice in a biographical musical. "She's very extraordinary," gushes Truman Capote. "She is one of the true phenomenons of today. My favorites are Bea Lillie and Billie Holiday, and she's the only one I've heard equal to them."

The span from Bea Lillie's light lyrics to Billie Holiday's blues is broad, but Barbra's strength is versatility. She is headed for an unprecedented triple crown of New York night life—hit stands in the basements, the barns and the boites. In the Greenwich Village basements, like the Bon Soir, where she started two years ago, intimacy is the key, and when Barbra sings "My Coloring Book," the audience feels as though it is eavesdropping on her most private thoughts. In the jazzy barns, like Basin Street East, where she is currently appearing, singers are usually fighting trumpets and drunks, but when Barbra belts "Cry Me a River," she cows everyone into stunned contentment. "People shut up," she says. "What can I tell you?" In the fancy boites, like the Persian Room, where she opens in the fall, singers become song stylists, and when Barbra bursts into "Happy Days Are Here Again," sunshine floods her funny face and it is as if no one had ever sung the trite ditty before. Between songs, she throws in sly patter—kidding herself and her audiences—and snappy, sometimes macabre short numbers: "You better not shout, you better not cry, you better not pout, I'm telling you why—Santa Claus is dead."

Young Kook: Miss Streisand has always had a weakness for the offbeat. As a teenager, she colored her hair to suit her mood. As a budding actress, she told Lee Strasberg that her favorite actress was Rita Hayworth. "I didn't want to study with him," she explains. As a show-stopper in *Wholesale*, she divorced herself from the play, reading *Mad* magazine between her numbers. When friendly gossip columnist Earl Wilson caught her at the stage door one night, she told him to stop following her around. "You're a stage-door Johnny," she hollered, the shout echoing down Shubert Alley.

During her rise, reporters introduced to her had the disconcerting feeling that they were interrupting in the middle of a conversation. A typical monologue would careen from malteds (she liked them) to lawsuits (she had them) to cut velvet (she wanted some) to perfume (she could identify any one at twenty paces). She wanted stardom so that she could get a Rolls-Royce and drive it in sneakers.

Old Foggy: She is now a star, at least in nightclubs and on Columbia Records, but she does not have the new Rolls. She also does not quite have the old call to nuttiness. "I'm calmer," she says. "I'm much more depressed. My rose-colored glasses are fogged. Nothing impresses me as it did then. I'm an old married woman [last year to *Wholesale* star Elliot Gould]. Being talked about doesn't matter any more."

As a star, she has her share of detractors. "If you maintain a standard of work in order not to get knocked down for not maintaining a standard of work, then you get knocked down for being a prima donna," she says. "Now that I'm accepted on a mass level, I'm starting to get torn down. People always want a scene stealer. That's democracy! Most people don't really know when I'm good or bad, that's the sickest part of it."

Streisand knows when she's right. "I feel powerful then," she says with a grand sweep of her hand. "I feel . . . I feel . . . like the queen." She is the first to admit that she doesn't look like the queen. Her hair is now being done by Mr. Kenneth, but her face is hard to take seriously, and her figure is often encased in an unflattering high-waisted gingham tent—leading rumorists to blurt in print that she is pregnant.

"I get worried," she says, about such false reports. "Maybe they know something I don't know."

28

BARBRA STREISAND: FOUR YEARS TO THE TOP
CBS Television press release, October 11, 1965

*B*arbra Streisand dreamed of fame when she was a child. At 23 she's the brightest name in show business, having climbed to the top in four short years. She's still rubbing the stardust out of her eyes.

"I can't believe it," she says when talking about her meteoric rise. But the credentials are gilt-edged.

Her first starring effort on television, the one-woman CBS Television Network special "My Name Is Barbra," was a smashing success and won her an Emmy award for excellence. Her records have been on the top-seller list since her initial Columbia LP album was issued in 1963. She has captured Broadway with her portrayal of the late comedienne Fanny Brice in the hit musical "Funny Girl."

The millions of Streisand devotees, who keep clamoring for more, are assured of seeing her name in lights for many years to come.

"My Name is Barbra" was her first show under terms of her long-term agreement with the Network. Her inimitable way with a song, be it the haunting interpretation of "Happy Days Are Here Again" or the defiant "Don't Rain on My Parade," has established Miss Streisand as one of the most original singers to come along.

The Streisand style is explained by the star this way:

"I sing songs I'm comfortable with."

Her manager, Martin Erlichman, maintains: "Barbra just follows her own instincts."

Miss Streisand, who was born in Brooklyn, quotes her mother for an early clue to her theatrical bent:

"My mother says I had lipstick smeared on my face and was acting on a dresser when I was 2. She caught me before I fell. Maybe that was the first time I actually acted."

As she was growing up, her desire to perform became stronger.

"When I was a kid—a poor one—I was certain I'd be famous one day," she says. "I didn't know how, but I used to dream about it. When I'd tell my mother about it, she would say, 'How can you be famous? You're too skinny.' "

But the dream persisted. At 14, Miss Streisand attended her first Broadway play, "The Diary of Anne Frank." She still remembers her reaction: "I thought I could go up on that stage and play any role without any trouble at all."

She was an honor student at Erasmus Hall High School and graduated with a 93 average, winning a medal for excellence in Spanish.

After a brief fling at summer stock, Miss Streisand won a talent contest shortly after her 18th birthday. This led to a singing engagement at the Bon Soir, a Greenwich Village night club. Her original two-week engagement became an 11-week run.

Her first New York stage appearance, in the off-Broadway revue "An Evening with Harry Stoones," lasted one evening (Oct. 21, 1961). But her next stage assignment, in the 1962 Broadway musical comedy "I Can Get It For You Wholesale," was more rewarding. Miss Streisand was greeted with glowing personal notices for her portrayal of the unloved secretary, Miss Marmelstein. She won the Best Supporting Actress award of the New York Drama Critics' Circle and a nomination for one of the theater's highest honors, the Antoinette Perry (Tony) Award.

This musical was lucky for Miss Streisand on another count. She married the leading man, Elliot Gould.

From the time "I Can Get It For You Wholesale" closed to her triumphant opening in "Funny Girl" March 26, 1964, Miss Streisand became one of the country's top stars via recordings, supper-club dates and television appearances. She has been a guest on the Ed Sullivan, Dinah Shore, Bob Hope and Garry Moore shows.

Miss Streisand credits her first television appearance to Orson Bean. "I had worked with him in a night club. He asked me to appear on the 'Tonight' show on April 5, 1961, while he was the substitute host. If it weren't for him, I might never have gotten any television program.

"That particular night was an exciting one for the entire Streisand family. My brother's wife had a baby, and my mother didn't know whether to go see her first grandchild or watch me on television. Luckily, she was able to do both," she recalls.

Miss Streisand and her husband live in a Manhattan apartment. The refrigerator is usually stocked with lots of coffee ice cream—one of Miss Streisand's favorite desserts.

THE JEANING OF BARBRA STREISAND
Grover Lewis
Rolling Stone magazine, June 24, 1971

*L*OS ANGELES—Holmby Hills, Humphrey Bogart's old neighborhood, is an enclave of the kind of profligate wealth amassed from such ventures as deep-bleed oil drilling, the pioneer sorties of the Hollywood dreammakers, and somebody else's stoop labor stooping and laboring in perpetuity. The streets are quiet, sloping and well patrolled by flint-eyed private security guards; the houses, more often than not, are immense anthems to the Early Chilidipper School of Southern California architecture, most of them hidden behind what looks suspiciously like electrified shrubbery.

Barbra Streisand's place is no exception. The rooms are massive, pin-neat, high-vaulted, gorged with Art Nouveau and Art Deco furnishings. In the music room connecting to a solarium which affords a view of an Olympic-size swimming pool, everything has its proper niche: the countless photos of her four-year-old son Jason (no pictures of her estranged husband Elliot Gould), an unopened pack of Sherman's Cigaretellos, neat stacks of books and magazines.

Along with the rest of America, Barbra herself is jeaning these days, head to heel. Dressed in matching denim jacket and flares with that unmistakable *de rigueur* patina of garments washed precisely once—the overall ensemble topped off by a bio-degradable denim sombrero—she whips into the sun room, sizes up the assembled talent, frowns at the sight of a working tape recorder, grimaces dourly at the unexpected presence of a photographer, then strides to the glass door opening on the patio to oversee two gardeners who are topping out some trees beyond the pool. Though it's early afternoon, the sky has already sickied over with yellowish schmaze endemic to Southern California. "There's never enough sun for the pool," she complains, sinking down at a white table and making a pretty face at the whirring tape machine. Abruptly, she swings around to a paid functionary: "I wanted to play that Carole King record today, David. It was on the turntable last night, and now it's gone. Do you suppose the cleaning girl took it?" Distractedly, she traces a finger along the soft line of deli-food chubbiness that rings her fetching jaw and sniffles into a handkerchief. "And to top everything off, I've got this shitty cold. I have to *record* tonight." Her clear hazel eyes blip with irritation.

"I'm not organized, you know. It's a life-long failing. Things like colds complicate everything, and I get furious. I don't like to be hampered by my body. There aren't enough hours in the day as it is. Also I don't do any exercises, and I'm terribly . . . I started playing tennis, you know, because that was a way to exercise. Maybe it was growing up in Brooklyn with a mother whose attitude was: 'Don't get your feet wet, you'll catch cold. Don't skip rope, you'll break a bone.' I guess that made me fearful of most things.

"I *am*, you know. You name it. I'm scared of it—skiing, hikes, coldness, water, heat, everything. I'm afraid of the world, probably. That's why I admire Jane Fonda—nothing fazes her. Bella Abzug, too, the congresswoman. But me, I'm scared of crowds, of people in general. That's why I stay here in my little house most of the time. Simple fear."

A black maid serves coffee. Barbra peers into her cup pensively.

"Being so scary—that's stupid of me, isn't it? So goddamn stupid. Then, too, I love to eat. I love to eat so much I have no will power about it. I always think, so what, so I'll get a little fat. Then I get fat. Oy!" Abruptly she puts on a smile like a tiara, then notices one of the gardeners motioning at her. "What does *he* want? I want him to cut off the top of that tree, is what I want him to do. God, I hate to have anything done, because there's always a discussion about it, and then if it's not felt out properly to begin with, it doesn't come off right. Tell the truth, I don't know how I get anything done. Hey, I must sound peculiar, huh?" Shaking her head, she laughs raucously.

"Is my music greening, is that the question? What does that mean? Oh. Well, I'm not so old, you know. Only 28. Have you heard *What About Today?* and *Stoney End?* I think those albums feature good music from good writers—John Lennon, Randy Newman, Paul Simon, Carole King. I truly admire people like those: they have a gift that I greatly lack.

"Look, I'm considered this kind of institution thing. I'm labeled, pigeonholed. I play for middle-class audiences in Vegas. I made those definitely establishment pictures—*Dolly, On a Clear Day, Funny Girl.* All of which tags me as a 'veteran performer.' But I ask you, 28—is that old? Is 28 all that old?

"Let me tell you about the last time I played Vegas. I didn't take any fancy gowns, no intro, no overture. Just walked on, didn't want any kind of star thing. I don't go for all that crap. It cheats people as an audience, and I'm truly not interested in it. On top of which I don't like to perform. That's true. I don't even like to be watched.

"Anyway, since I get nervous in places like Vegas, it occurred to me to do this funny little routine—actually telling the audience about my hangup. The point was, you shouldn't rely on emotional crutches. It was almost a sermon—no crutches, people; crutches are a no-no. Then at the end, I'd take out a joint and light it. First, just faking it. Then I started lighting live joints, passing them around to the band—you know. It was *great*—it relieved all my tensions. And I ended up with the greatest supply of grass ever. Other acts up and down the Strip heard about what I was doing—Little Anthony and the Imperials, people like that—and started sending me the best dope in the world. I never ran out. Hmm . . . I wonder if I should tell that story."

She drums a nervous tattoo on the tabletop, glancing at the tape machine as if she hopes it will self-destruct. In seven seconds, it doesn't and she flashes another radiant smile.

"Yeah, well people have a lot of misconceptions about me, you see. Some of which I resent. Like the 'star' business. *I* don't think of myself as a star, my *friends* don't think of me as a star. The fact is, a large part of me is pure nebbish—plain, dull, uninteresting. There's a more flamboyant part, too, obviously. But, listen, I'm still surprised, even embarrassed, when people recognize me in public. People will crowd into your booth at a restaurant, stop you on the street, all that crap. Well, I'm not a person who needs people—not *those* goddamn pushy people anyway. Or maybe somebody will only *think* he recognizes me"—here, her long, tapering fingers punch out the story like a late-breaking wire dispatch—"and say, 'Oh, wow, I know *you*. You're . . . why, you're *Lainie Kazan!*'"

She laughs explosively, squirms in her chair, takes a sip of luke-cold coffee. Outside the two workmen are ghostly blurs in the haze-shrouded tops of the trees.

"The real truth about me . . . I'm lazy. Lazy to the bone. Is that contradictory? Well, I'm contradictory, then. Also a mother, an actress, a singer, and I have responsibilities and commitments in all those capacities. Lazy, though . . . God, I never even used to make my bed when I was a kid in Brooklyn. Still, I had this great need to be accepted, and that gave me a great drive. Before I made it, though, my life was my own, and I always had this feeling of—dignity. If I hadn't made it pretty early, I'd probably have been a fashion designer, something like that. But I was accepted quite easily. I never had to struggle, except in myself. See, I have—*had*—great will power. I thought ever since I was about seven that I was going to die, and I lived my life on that premise.

"Read a book about cancer, developed all the imaginary symptoms for cancer, like that. But I never told anybody—it was a secret thing. Also, I have supersonic hearing due to a deviated septum and . . . umm, all those things probably contributed to my success. Do I mean it was fated? Well, hmm. I'm a Taurus, but I only believe in that when it's convenient."

She leans forward intently, arms akimbo.

"See, it's hard to explain, but it has to do with *reality*. I like to talk about what's real, involve myself in projects that're real. I'm going to do a movie soon with Peter Bogdanovich, and that'll hopefully turn out to have some of the value I mean. The youth movement in this country . . ." she hurries past the phrase as if it's embarrassing, which it more or less is—". . . that stuff's for real. I don't mean burning colleges, drastic tactics. That's as despicable as Nixon-Agnew. But so *many* kids are trying to change the system by getting involved in the processes of change, and it's fantastic; things're changing, we're making progress.

"I care about people who care. I care about my day-to-day friends, whom I don't care to discuss. Would I care to comment about Mr. Gould? What do you mean? Anything to say? Just in general? Mmm . . . *No*.

"But let me tell you about my son Jason. A tough cookie, extremely bright. He's always had a fantastic sense of words and analogy. I'll say, 'Isn't that girl cute?, she looks French.' He'll say, 'Yeah, cute like French toast.'

35

"Once I was talking to him on a very simplistic level and he soared right above my bullshit and came straight to the point. He's so open, he knows so much, and he's uncorrupted by phony attitudes. I don't want to put my crap in his head any more than I can help, but I'm resigned to the fact that there's no way I can *not* screw him up."

Looking bemused, she rises and walks over to the glass door. Outside, the workmen sever an enormous branch, and it arcs slowly through the air, hitting the sheer slope beyond the pool in a dead slide all the way down Barbra's very own Holmby Hill.

That evening, in the depot-sized master studio at Columbia Records in downtown L.A., Barbra's jeaning has done a fast fade in favor of regalia more suitable for a queen of symphonic pop: she's wearing a svelte blue pants suit, a crimson, knee-length leather smock and matching street-boy cap. The effect is not unlike the over-ripe brilliance of out-of-tune color TV. "Doesn't she look *smashing*?" an aging hipster PR man enthuses, watching from the control booth as she threads a skittish path through the maze of music stands to her mike-side perch on a high stool.

"This'll be a take on 'The Summer Knows,'" Richard Perry, the session's producer intones over the talk-back hookup. "We're gonna play 35 through 38, then Bob-ra comes in, right?" On cue, Bob-ra comes in, indeed, sounding just like herself—sounding, in fact, just like the prominent-nosed teen-aged girl with that inimitable tendency toward lyrical over-kill who sang "Happy Days Are Here Again" and "My Coloring Book" and "People" all those years ago. "Christ," Tom Donohue wheezes, lowering his hulk by stages into a low-slung couch, "that's 43 musicians out there, baby—more than anybody else uses in a year." Somebody asks Donohue what's his connection with the session. He shrugs: "Ah, Tuesday's a slow night in L.A."

After the music ends, Barbra sweeps into the booth, looking edgy, spring-tight: "The ending leaves more than something to be desired, Dick. I don't know how to explain in words what's wrong with the sounds, but . . ." While she and Perry confer in intense *sotto voce* off to one side, the aging hipster leans forward confidentially and taps one of the visitors on the arm: "Doesn't she sound terrific? Barbra's only 28, you know. People have the impression she's much older. But that's not old, do you think . . . 28? Why, that's two years younger than Dylan."

STREISAND AS SCHWARZKOPF
Glenn Gould
High Fidelity Magazine, May 1976

The voice that is "one of the natural wonders of the age" confronts The Masters.

I'm a Streisand freak and make no bones about it. With the possible exception of Elisabeth Schwarzkopf, no vocalist has brought me greater pleasure or more insight into the interpreter's art.

Fourteen years ago, an acetate of her first disc, *The Barbra Streisand Album*, was being smuggled from cubicle to cubicle at CBS; I caught a preview, and laughed. Not at it, certainly—her eager mentor, Martin Erlichman, was simultaneously doing his own number in an adjacent office and it wouldn't have been good corporate policy in any case. And not always *with* it either—though it was obvious even then that parody would play a vital role in Streisand's work. What happened, rather, was that I broke into a sort of Cheshire-cat grin that seems to strike its own bargain with my facial muscles, deigning to exercise them only when confronted with unique examples of the rite of re-creation.

Sometimes, this curious tic is caught off guard by novelty (Walter Carlos' Moog meditations on the third and fourth *Brandenburgs*, for example, or the Swingle Singers' scat-scanning of the ninth fugue from the *Art of*). Sometimes, it cracks up over repertoire for which I have no real affection. (I always felt that I could live without the Chopin concertos and managed to until Alexis Weissenberg dusted the cobwebs from Mme. Sand's salon and made those works a contemporary experience.) Sometimes, inappropriately perhaps, it surfaces in the presence of a work for which poker-faced solemnity is considered *de rigeur*. (Hermann Scherchen's boogie-beat *Messiah* was, for me, one of the great revelations of the early LP era.) Sometimes it conveys my relief upon discovering that a puzzle I had thought insoluble has fallen into place. (Strauss's *Metamorphosen*, for example, is a work I have loved, on paper, as a concept, for nearly thirty years but which I had long since written off as a vehicle for twenty-three wayward strings in search of a six-four chord. All that changed a couple of years ago when I first heard Karajan's magisterial recording. For weeks, night after night, on occasion two or three times per—I'm not exaggerating—I played that disc, passed through the eyes-uplifted-in-wonder stage, went well beyond the catch-in-throat-and-tingle-on-the-spinal-cord phase and, at last, stood on the threshold of . . . laughter.) I have the same reaction to practically everything conducted by Willem Mengelberg or Leopold Stokowski and always—well, almost always—to Barbra Streisand.

For me, the Streisand voice is one of the natural wonders of the age, an instrument of infinite diversity and timbral resource. It is not, to be sure, devoid of problem areas—which is an observation at least as perspicacious as the comment that a harpsichord is not a piano or, if you insist, vice versa. Streisand always has had problems with the upper third of the stave—breaking the C-sharp barrier in low gear is chief among them—but space does not permit us to count the ways in which, with ever-increasing ingenuity, she has turned this impediment to advantage. I cannot, however, let the occasion pass without mention of a moment of special glory—the "Nothing, nothing, nothing" motif, securely focused on D flat and C natural, from the final seconds of that Puccini-like blockbuster, "He Touched Me."

In truth, though, one does not look to Streisand as one looks to Ella Fitzgerald or, as some will have it—I'm not sure that I will but that's another story—Cleo Laine, for vocal pyrotechnics. The lady can sing up a storm upon demand, but she is not a ballad-belter in the straightforward "this is a performance" manner of the admirable Shirley Bassey. With Streisand, who relates to Bassey as Daniel Barenboim to Loren Maazel, one becomes engaged by process, by a seemingly limitless array of available options. Hers is, indeed, a manner of much greater intimacy, but an intimacy that (astonishingly, for this repertoire) is never overtly in search of sexual contact. Streisand is consumed by nostalgia; she can make of the torchiest lyric an intimate memoir, and it would never occur to her to employ the "I'll meet you precisely 51 percent of the way" piquancy of, say, Helen Reddy, much less the "I won't bother to speak up 'cause you're already spellbound, aren't you?" routine of Peggy Lee.

My private fantasy about Streisand (about Schwarzkopf, too, for that matter) is that all her greatest cuts result from dressing-room-run-throughs in which (presumably to the accompaniment of a prerecorded orchestral mix) Streisand puts on one persona after another, tries out probable throw-away lines, mugs accompanying gestures to her own reflection, samples registrational couplings (super the street-urchin four-foot pipe on the so-phisticated-lady 16-foot) and, in general, performs for her own amusement in a world of Borgesian mirrors (Jorge-Luis, not Victor) and word-invention.

Like Schwarzkopf, Streisand is one of the great italicizers; no phrase is left solely to its own devices, and the range and diversity of her expressive gift is such that one is simply unable to chart an *a priori* stylistic course on her behalf. Much of the *Affekt* of intimacy—indeed, the sensation of eavesdropping on a private moment not yet wholly committed to its even-tual public profile—is a direct result of our inability to anticipate her in-tentions. As but one example, Streisand can take a lightweight Satie-satire like Dave Grusin's "A Child Is Born," find in it two descending scales (Hypodorian and Lydian, respectively), and wring from that routine cross-relation a moment of heartbreakingly beautiful intensity. Improbable as the comparison may seem, it is, I think, close kin to Schwarzkopf's unforget-table musings upon the closing soliloquy of Strauss's *Capriccio* and, in my opinion, the bulk of Streisand's output richly deserves the compliment implied.

Unfortunately, the present disc is one of those "almost-always" excep-tions. Another that comes to mind is the irritating sing-in for the Now—or, rather, Then—generation, *What About Today?*, produced in 1969. Un-like that latter package, however, *Classical Barbra* is obviously not intended to placate the *Zeitgeist*. Other than as a curio, it can hardly be expected to attract musicology majors, its tight, pop-style pickup (personally, I adore it!) will almost certainly alienate the art-song set, and its contents over-all will quite probably turn off the casual M.O.R. shopper to boot.

So, a measure of courage is involved here; Streisand has obviously risked a good deal in order to cater to the boundless curiosity of her hard-core fans, and, if only out of gratitude, we should make clear that, if this is not really a good album, it is certainly not a bad one either. It is con-siderate to a fault of the presumed prerequisites of the repertoire it surveys and, as such, to take the most obvious comparative route, puts to shame the ill-considered renditions of Broadway show-stoppers offered by such talk-show groupies from the classical field as Beverly Sills, Roberta Peters, or, occasionally, Maureen Forrester. (One should probably exempt Eileen Farrell, who really did "have a right to sing the blues.")

But it's the presumption of those prerequisites that causes problems. Nothing in this album is insensitive or unmusical—unless it's the gratuitous reverb slopped into the Handel orchestra tracks, which reaches a peak of stylistic defiance at the end of both excerpts where an engineer's quick pull on the pot only makes us more aware of its excremental presence. Throughout, though, Streisand appears awed by the realization that she is now face to face with The Masters. The entire album is served up at a reverential range of mezzo-piano to mezzo-forte, and none of the cuts could be described as "up-tempo." Notwithstanding the fact that the lady is the most adroit patter-song purveyor of our time ("Piano Practice," "Minute Waltz"), this predilection for an unvaried sequence of andante-grazioso intermezzi is not unique to this disc. It turned up as early in her career as *The Third Barbra Streisand Album*, but was not then allied, as in the present instance, to an austere dynamic compression.

It is also virtually a one-stop performance; Streisand pulls out her choir-boy-innocent 8-foot and settles in for the duration. This is, to be sure, one of her most effective registrations and, when mated with appropriate repertoire, produces spellbinding results. For Orff's "*In Trutina*," Streisand, using the fastest vibrato in the west and the most impeccable intonation this side of Maria Stader's prime, provides a reading second to none in terms of vocal security while stripping this rather vapid air of its customary theatrical accouterments. More to the point, perhaps, she turns in the only current version possessed of exactly the right Book of Hours–like accommodation to the text.

In the "*Berceuse*" (from Canteloube's *Songs of the Auvergne*), Streisand cannot match the suave production of De Los Angeles but, on its own folklike terms, her performance is quite extraordinarily touching. She does well with Debussy, too, and if Eileen Farrell, who also opened a Columbia collection with "*Beau soir*," stakes out her territory as a sophisticated Parisienne, Streisand replies, not ineffectively, as a Marseillian gamine.

It's in the German repertoire that Streisand runs aground. In Schu-

41

mann's "*Mondnacht*" she keeps a maddening cool during the final stanza, plodding relentlessly through "*Und meine Seele spannte, weit ihre Flügel aus.*" In Wolf's "*Verschwiegene Liebe,*" she simply sets aside her unique powers of characterization, keeping no secrets and wearing no veils.

About the most that can be said of her "*Lascia ch'io pianga*" from *Rinaldo* is that it is a model of analytic clarity when set beside the glissando-ridden 1906 production of Mme. Ernestine Schumann-Heink. Streisand delivers it according to the approved Royal Academy (1939) method—glissandos were out by then but ornaments had not yet been invented. (Ironically, it is left to Alfred Deller's superb collaborator, Eileen Poulter, to turn in the definitively Streisandesque version of this air.)

I do not, however, want to leave the impression that Streisand should give up on "the classics." Indeed, I'm convinced that she has a great "classical" album in her. She simply needs to rethink the question of repertoire and to dispense with the yoke of respectability which burdens the present production.

My own prescription for a Streisand dream album would include Tudor lute songs (she'd be sensational in Dowland), Mussorgsky's *Sunless* cycle and, as *pièce de résistance*—providing she'll pick up a handbook or two on baroque ornamentation—Bach's Cantata No. 54. To date, in my experience, the most committed performance of this glorious piece was on a CBC television show in 1962. It featured the remarkable countertenor Russell Oberlin and a squad of strings from the Toronto Symphony. It also involved a harpsichordist/conductor of surpassing modesty who has requested anonymity; I am, however, assured by his agent that if Ms. Streisand would like to take a crack at *Wiederstehe doch der Sünde*, and if Columbia would like to take a hint, he's available.

STREISAND'S 20-YEAR BLITZ
Paul Grein
Billboard magazine, April 16, 1983

*T*wenty years ago this week, the debut album by a promising 21-year-old singer from Brooklyn made its first appearance on the Billboard charts. The album would go on to hit the top 10 and win two Grammys; the singer would go on to become the most celebrated female vocalist of her generation, and to rank with Judy Garland and Ella Fitzgerald as the top female pop singer of the century.

That singer, it should go without saying, is Barbra Streisand, who has been a leading force on the pop charts for most of the two decades since the release of "The Barbra Streisand Album."

A grand total of 38 Streisand albums have hit the charts over the years, including nine soundtracks and two original cast albums. Fully 27 of these releases were certified gold, and 18 shot into the top 10. Streisand's singles track record, after a slow start, is also impressive: 34 chart hits, including seven that went gold and 11 that cracked the top 10.

But one measure of Streisand's tremendous popularity is that she's conquered so many different charts during her career. "No More Tears," a 1979 duet with Donna Summer, was a top 20 black hit and also logged four weeks at No. 1 on the disco chart. (And that wasn't Streisand's first disco hit: "Main Event"/"Fight" had climbed to 13 on the disco chart that summer, and "Shake Me, Wake Me" garnered club plays in 1974.)

"You Don't Bring Me Flowers," Streisand's 1978 duet with Neil Diamond, spent two months in the lower reaches of the country chart; 1976's "Classical Barbra" logged four months in the top 10 on the classical chart. Streisand has also placed 47 single hits on the adult contemporary chart, including 27 that cracked the top 10.

One of the most lasting effects of Streisand's success has been the way she helped open the door to album acceptance for female artists. Streisand was the only female solo artist in the industry to earn a gold album in '64 or '65; ten years later, in '74 and '75, a total of 16 female soloists notched gold albums.

Streisand's success in her first three years of recording was little short of astonishing. Between April 1963 and April 1966, eight Streisand albums cracked the charts (including the "Funny Girl" cast album on Capitol). Incredibly, all eight went top 10 and were certified, gold, while five were nominated for the Grammy for album of the year.

Streisand also won the Grammy for female pop vocalist for three years running from '63 to '65, and swept the NARM Award for best-selling female vocalist for four straight years, through '66. In fact, one indication of Streisand's amazing longevity is suggested by the names of her male counterparts in those awards. The Grammys those years went to Jack Jones, Louis Armstrong and Frank Sinatra; the NARM trophies to Andy Williams, Elvis Presley and Dean Martin.

But after '66, Streisand's recording career hit a prolonged lull, as she concentrated her time and energies on establishing herself as a film star. Except for the "Funny Girl" soundtrack (1968), Streisand went without a gold album for five full years, from "Color Me Barbra" in April, 1966 to "Stoney End" in April, 1971.

But one of the most interesting aspects of Streisand's career has been the way she's always been able to bounce back from intermittent lulls. Her re-emergence with the "Stoney End" album is the most dramatic example, coming as it did on the heels of her low-charting soundtracks to "On a Clear Day You Can See Forever" and "The Owl And The Pussycat." In much the same way, Streisand's 1973 smash "The Way We Were" came right on top of (and thus helped mask) the failure of her soundtrack to the tv special "Barbra Streisand . . . And Other Musical Instruments."

The most significant development in Streisand's career over the past decade has been her belated but dramatic acceptance at pop radio. As late as January 1977, Streisand had cracked Billboard's top 30 with only three single hits: "People," "Stoney End" and "The Way We Were." But late that month "Evergreen" became Streisand's fourth top 30 hit, and she's since collected 10 more.

This doubtless explains why Streisand's first greatest hits album (released in 1970) peaked at 32 on the pop chart and took nearly 15 months

44

to go gold, while her second hit-studded collection (in 1978) raced to No. 1 in six weeks and went gold and platinum on release.

Still, Streisand has one of the best batting averages of any major leaguer in pop. Of the 27 pure Streisand albums issued by Columbia over the years (discounting movie soundtracks and cast albums), a remarkable 21 have gone gold. And four of those non-gold albums ("Je M'Appelle Barbra," "Simply Streisand," "A Happening in Central Park" and "What About Today") were successive releases during Streisand's late '60s record slump. The two other albums to fall short of gold were also exceptional cases: "Classical Barbra" and the "Musical Instruments" tv soundtrack.

Streisand is posted at number 60 on this week's pop album chart with "Memories," the 1981 release that was her seventh consecutive album to be certified platinum (and her fourth in a row to go gold and platinum simultaneously). Streisand's next album release will be the "Yentl" soundtrack, featuring a score by Michel Legrand and lyrics by Marilyn and Alan Bergman. It's scheduled for November release.

45

BARBRA IN BILLBOARD: A CHART DISCOGRAPHY

RELEASE DATE	TITLE	HIGHEST CHART POSITION	WEEKS ON CHART	CERTIFIED GOLD/PLATINUM
Apr 62	I Can Get It For You Wholesale (Original Cast)	125	5	——
May 62	Pins and Needles	——	——	——
Feb 63	The Barbra Streisand Album	8	101	(G) Oct 64
Aug 63	The Second Barbra Streisand Album	2	74	(G) May 64
Feb 64	The Third Album	5	74	(G) Feb 65
Apr 64	Funny Girl (Original Cast)	2	51	(G) Sep 64
Sep 64	People	1	84	(G) Mar 65
May 65	My Name is Barbra	2	68	(G) Dec 65
Oct 65	My Name is Barbra Two	2	48	(G) Jan 66
Mar 66	Color Me Barbra	3	36	(G) Apr 66
Mar 66	Harold Sings Arlen (With Friend)	——	——	——
Oct 66	Je m'Appelle Barbra	5	29	——
Oct 67	Simply Streisand	12	23	——
Oct 67	A Christmas Album	1	(NA)	(G) Jan 76
Jul 68	Funny Girl (Soundtrack)	12	108	(G) Dec 68
Sep 68	A Happening in Central Park	30	20	——
Jul 69	What About Today?	31	40	——
Dec 69	Hello, Dolly! (Soundtrack)	49	33	——
Dec 69	Barbra Streisand's Greatest Hits	32	30	(G) May 71
Jul 70	On a Clear Day (Soundtrack)	108	24	——

Dec 70	The Owl and the Pussycat (Soundtrack)	186	6	——
Feb 71	Stoney End	10	29	(G) Apr 71
Aug 71	Barbra Joan Streisand	11	26	(G) Dec 71
Oct 72	Live Concert at the Forum	19	27	(G) Feb 73
Oct 73	Barbra Streisand and Other Musical Instruments (Soundtrack)	64	16	——
Jan 74	The Way We Were	1	31	(G) Feb 74
Jan 74	The Way We Were (Soundtrack)	20	15	(G) Sep 75
Oct 74	Butterfly	13	21	(G) Jan 75
Mar 75	Funny Lady (Soundtrack)	6	25	(G) Sep 75
Oct 75	Lazy Afternoon	12	20	(G) Apr 76
Feb 76	Classical Barbra	46	14	——
Nov 76	A Star is Born (Soundtrack)	1	51	(P) Jan 77
Jun 77	Streisand Superman	3	25	(P) Aug 77
May 78	Songbird	12	27	(P) Aug 78
Nov 78	Greatest Hits, Volume Two	1	85	(P) Nov 78
Jun 79	The Main Event (Soundtrack)	20	18	(P) Sep 79
Oct 79	Wet	7	26	(P) Feb 80
Sep 80	Guilty	1	49	(P) Nov 80
Nov 81	Memories	10	70	(P) Jan 82

THE PRICE OF FAME
Robert Sandall
The London Times, April 24, 1994

The seats were more expensive than at Covent Garden. But note for note, ROBERT SANDALL wanted a little more from Barbra Streisand.

*I*n her floorlength coat and floppy hat she looked more like a middle-aged hippie chick than the highest paid pop diva in the world, but there was no mistake who was speaking: "Listen you people, my name is pronounced with a soft 's', like the stuff on the beach. Stry-sand."

The singer-actress with the long wavy nose and the no-nonsense Brooklyn accent smiled patiently last week, while a gaggle of British paparazzi at the photo call, some still braying for clear shots of "Miss Streizund," got a brief glimpse of the lady's legendary perfectionism—or obsessive persnicketiness—where her professionalism is concerned.

Staff at the nearby Wembley Arena saw rather more of this character trait. Before Barbra (no "a") Streisand gave her first London concert in 28 years last Wednesday night, the 12,000-seat concrete venue had to be carpeted throughout, either to make it "less draughty" or to improve the acoustics, depending on which paper you read. Few can know what other demands were placed upon her conductor, Marvin Hamlisch, and his 60-piece orchestra—locked in rehearsal with the star for six days before these London shows—but when you perform in public as infrequently as Miss Streisand, nothing escapes your scrutiny. "There's a part of me that sits at a scoring session and goes, 'No, no, no, the oboe goes *here*,'" she told *Vanity Fair* in 1991, adding firmly, "I don't lose those arguments."

Streisand's reappearance here, for the first time since she opened Styne and Merrill's musical *Funny Girl* in the West End in 1966, caused a sensation that not even Madonna in her brashest moments could have equaled. No stunt pulled by La Ciccone or her minders has stirred more public interest than the prices charged by Barbra Streisand and promoter Harvey Goldsmith for her four concerts. The mighty Pavarotti has never made such extravagant demands on our wallets. The best seats cost £260, making them the most expensive non-charity concert tickets ever in the UK; the cheapest were £48.50. All sold out within hours of going on sale last month. Touts, we heard, had since been asking £500 a ticket. Streisand herself would fly home an estimated £5 million richer. In a country still struggling to shake off economic depression, the news that her British fans were prepared to stake the price of a holiday, or a down payment on a car, for two hours in her presence was food not just for thought, but for serious wonderment. Even Streisand's mother was reported to have recently asked her daughter, "Why do they pay you that much to sing?"

Part of the secret lies in the sheer scarcity of her live performances. Though she started out as a teenager singing in gay clubs and off-Broadway revues in New York City in the early 1960s, by the end of the decade Streisand had closeted herself in Hollywood. She walked out of the London run of *Funny Girl*—the show about an early Broadway star, Fanny Brice, which made her a worldwide household name—after she became pregnant by Elliot Gould. The following year, on the eve of a vast concert in Central Park, she received a death threat from Palestinian terrorists angered by her public support of Israel during the Six-Day War with Egypt. Understandably panicked, Streisand stumbled over a few lines in front of a crowd of 135,000. The irritation and shame this caused drove her away from the stage and into the arms of the filmmakers. Only during the past year has she emerged from Garbo-esque seclusion. When asked last week why she had decided to "come back to perform in Britain," Streisand looked genuinely puzzled. "What do you mean back?" she said. "I haven't been anywhere."

Well, she has been to the movies. A steady stream of goodish-to-middling pictures in the 1970s saw her increasingly separate her music and acting: genial comedies such as *What's Up, Doc?* and *For Pete's Sake* established Streisand as a sassier, more streetwise character than the gawky loser who sang "Second Hand Rose." By 1976 and the release of her best-remembered film, a re-make of *A Star Is Born*, the world more or less divided up into those who felt that Barbra Streisand really was a New York

Jewish re-incarnation of Judy Garland, and those who distrusted her infatuation with old music and old film stars, and disliked her self-indulgent preoccupation with the trappings of her own celebrity.

For the next decade and a half, Streisand's career drifted on to stellar autopilot. The critics would rubbish her movies, and poke fun at the big name duets. The fans, meanwhile, grew both in number and in the intensity of their devotion. Her album sales in the 1980s exceeded those of the hits of the 1960s. As feminist ideas percolated into the mainstream, Streisand's enormous success and single-minded insistence on taking control of all aspects of her professional life appealed strongly to women: by the end of the 1970's she was directing, writing songs, producing and acting, all to her own specifications. One of the young acolytes applying to her for work was a struggling actress called Madonna Ciccone, of whom Streisand said later, "I was knocked out by her *chutzpah*."

Just as attractive to her growing female audience was Streisand's apparent ordinariness. Though she likes to show off her shapely legs from time to time, in the canon of female superstars Streisand comes across as far more glamorously challenged than most. She has always resisted taking the Californian option of having that extraordinary nose fixed. To judge from the sorts of things her British fans have been quoted as saying recently, she is approvingly felt to be "insecure," unlucky in love or even, as one tabloid headline writer phrased it, "Adored and Alone." The list of Streisand's former boyfriends, however, hardly endorses that: anybody whose name has been romantically linked with Elliot Gould, Warren Beatty, Ryan O'Neal, Steven Spielberg, Pierre Trudeau, Omar Sharif, Don Johnson, Richard Gere and, most recently, Andre Agassi, makes a pretty unconvincing wallflower.

But the lack of a husband, and that oft-quoted remark—"Objects are less disappointing than people"—have helped to spread the doctrine that Streisand is, at root, an unhappy soul. The sale of a few million dollars' worth of her worldly goods at auction in New York last month further stoked rumors of emotional and spiritual discontent. Her acknowledged interest in New Age psychology, and in books with titles such as *Homecoming: Reclaiming and Championing Your Inner Child*, are viewed, on this side of the Atlantic anyway, as clear signs that Streisand has never recovered from the tragedy of her father's death while she was still a baby.

The presentation of last Wednesday's show involved plenty of psycho-babble and child championing, too, though fortunately for those in the audience who didn't live in California much of it was handled with a light touch. Streisand did sound quite serious when she prefaced "On A Clear Day" with an explanation of how she had spent several thousand dollars on therapy before she learned to sing the song properly; but coming as this did at the end of the first half of a show strung around a running gag about long-winded and insensitive analysts, the implication was that the shrinks might have been overcharging her.

If Streisand's stage patter was never less than slick, her music was so well-oiled that the big emotions tended to slip past in a warm orchestral haze. The discovery that the lyrics to all these songs were being flashed up on autocue out in the auditorium served as a reminder that Streisand is no method actress. And the effect of high, cholesterol ballads such as "As If We Never Said Goodbye" and "The Way We Were" tended rather to celebrate the singer and the occasion of her return to live performance than to explore the nuances of the song.

This is not to deny that Streisand is a remarkable vocalist. While she was never formally trained, she has gifts for natural phrasing, and the superb clarity and agility with which she dispatched the old favorites fully justified Quincy Jones's memorable compliment about her "Stradivarius of a voice." But this distinguished instrument sometimes sounded rather crowded by Hamlisch and his enormous orchestra seated at the back.

Judged purely as a show, Streisand's Wembley debut was a fair success, and a multi-media spectacle which went at least part of the way towards justifying the exorbitant ticket prices. The set—a white mansion adorned with swags of white satin—looked nothing if not expensive, as, in a slightly less showy way, did Streisand's two outfits: a black-and-white ballgown which she wore until half-time, then a white three-piece suit.

As a two-hour summary of a meticulously well-managed career in show business, this was fine, and the audience was ecstatic throughout. The flaws only showed up if you went looking for any insight into the personality of Streisand herself, a woman who decided 28 years ago that playing the funny

52

girl with a heart of gold and a great voice is quite sufficient to keep the customers satisfied. But at current prices, some may begin to feel the lack of warmth which lies at the heart of the phenomenon called Barbra Streisand.

THE LAST OF HER KIND REMAINS A MYSTERY
Chris Willman
Los Angeles Times, September 22, 1991

BARBRA STREISAND
"Just for the Record . . ."
Columbia

What hath psychologist John Bradshaw wrought? His best-selling "inner child" reclamation theories reach their inevitable apotheosis on Barbra Streisand's version of "You'll Never Know" at the end of her massive new four-volume career retrospective.

On this old standard, the Barbra who is now in her late 40's duets with 13-year-old Barbra, courtesy of a scratchy acetate and modern technology. (The spooky effect is *à la* Nat and Natalie Cole, only through the looking glass instead of beyond the grave.)

Hearing the adult lovingly croon "you'll never know how much I miss you" to the child (and reading her liner notes about "coming to terms with ourselves by accepting . . . the child who still lives inside us") won't make Streisand any less of an easy target for detractors who make an on-going point of trying to prick her celebrated ego.

Yet finally the "duet" doesn't seem quite so narcissistic as all that, perhaps because the listener, too, after taking in these 4½ hours of material, can join Streisand in missing her younger, more defined self—along with the bygone musical era that produced her as the last of a breed.

And one reason America's favorite "funny girl" of yore seems so missable is that—illusion or not—she seemed knowable then, much more so than the powerful and publicly polite but slightly removed figure we see and hear so infrequently today.

At times as much an audio documentary of her professional life as a musical collection, "Just For The Record . . ." offers the fan many "personal" moments, if few truly revealing ones.

With her chart successes already well-documented on a series of greatest-hits albums over the years, this superbly designed box set admirably stresses unreleased material to the point that the recognizable versions of her standards easily take a back seat to the curios. Guest appearances on TV shows and awards show speeches are interspersed with live and studio recordings that never made it out of the vault, most of them more than worthy of the light of day.

But as the set progresses chronologically from the early '60s to the late '80s, Streisand herself slips more out of focus—not so much a fault of the collection itself as a reflection of the fact that she's had trouble relating to and finding a place in the encroaching rock era.

Maybe that's why the adult Barbra remains such a mystery.

As a singer of show tunes, Streisand is consummate, the major influence of her own generation and all the green theater majors that have succeeded her.

The first two volumes here—both devoted to her '60s work—are a delight, full of transition and growth even as Streisand stuck with what was clearly her element. The brassy musical comedian who made her mark as the show-stopping supporting player "Miss Marmelstein" (in the 1962 Broadway production "I Can Get It For You Wholesale") and can be heard developing into the more sensitive and controlled balladic interpreter who wraps up the decade with "On A Clear Day (You Can See Forever)."

The transition between zaniness and sobriety was exemplified almost literally in the lyrics of "Funny Girl," in which, as Fanny Brice—still her defining role as a star—Streisand acknowledges being good for a laugh but wants to be loved as a woman. She had versatility but, thanks to theater and the movies, she had even more of a persona.

Unfortunately, Streisand's peak coincided with the end of the era of film musicals. Since the trio she made in the late '60s ("Funny Girl," "Hello Dolly," "On A Clear Day"), she has starred in only three more ("Funny Lady," "A Star Is Born" and "Yentl").

On the pop side in the '70s and '80s, she groped often and with some difficulty for direction—though you wouldn't necessarily know it from this collection, which wisely skips over the missteps.

*   *   *

55

Among this massive undertaking, which includes more than 80 songs (counting medleys) on its four cassettes or CDs, a whopping total of *two* numbers are in a contemporary pop-rock mode: Laura Nyro's "Stoney End," her 1970 break from show-biz convention to attempt a rollicking Carole King style, and "Guilty," her 1980 duet with Bee Gee Barry Gibb.

Representative? Hardly. Streisand recorded album after album of light rock-oriented material, even venturing into disco with a hit duet with Donna Summer, little of which is to be found—or, frankly, terribly missed—here.

At the time of releasing her smash throwback "The Broadway Album" in '85, Streisand finally confessed her utter disdain for rock, which, while certainly narrow to the extreme, was at least a welcome concession she'd realized her manner of interpretation wasn't cut out for its very different demands.

But the exclusion of Streisand's many flirtations with passing mainstream pop styles means that the third and fourth volumes here—representing the '70s and '80s, respectively—are heavily laden with Barbra doing what Barbra now does best: ballads, most perfectly exemplified by the 1979 zenith, "Evergreen."

It's hard to find fault with too many of the individual selections (even if, unlike Streisand, you don't necessarily believe that Alan and Marilyn Bergman are the pre-eminent lyricists of our time). But digesting all this mounting easy-listening *en masse* isn't so easy on a listener as the box's earlier, more theatrical stretches.

Still, the tantalizing outtakes set down for the first time here stretch across all four volumes: Pre-stardom TV appearances with Johnny Carson, Garry Moore and Mike Wallace, all presciently commending what the world would soon know . . . on Judy Garland's variety show, a long, Sweeney Sisters–like medley with the host . . . an early nightclub medley that enjoyably segues for no apparent reason from "Cry Me A River" to "Who's Afraid of the Big Bad Wolf?" . . . a long-buried, nicely done companion piece to "The Way We Were," titled "The Way We Weren't" . . . and Frank Loesser's "Warm All Over," a preview of a future Streisand show-tunes project, an apparent sequel to her "Broadway Album."

Just as easy to compile are a list of documentary moments the true faithful might cherish but the casual fan could do without: Lengthy excerpts from a 1969 Friar's Club tribute (including Don Rickles affectionately telling Streisand's mother, "Your daughter is a dummy") . . . inconsequential dialogue from "A Star Is Born" . . . her memorable first Oscar acceptance speech ("Hello, gorgeous") followed by less memorable thank-yous at the Emmys and Grammys . . . a clumsy duet with Burt Bacharach of "Close to You" . . . and a benign yet bizarre long-distance chat about maternal instincts with then–Prime Minister Golda Meir, from the '79 special "A Salute to Israel at 30."

The portrait of Streisand that emerges from all this is of someone who wants to be liked and someone who wants to remain a little vague. A workhorse is her early years, the diva wields her clout more slowly and carefully now, appearing almost never and only for charity (the 1986 "One Voice," to help finance half a dozen threatened liberal Democrats), turning out films at the recent rate of two per decade, and making fewer and fewer records.

This may be less a function of laziness than the fact that dream projects are burdensome to get under way, even for such a Hollywood heavyweight.

Other than the liner-note applause for a liberal Congress and some asides about how her feminism inspired her to film "Yentl" and "Up The Sandbox," and a few old nuzzling–Jon Peters booklet snapshots, though, there are few peeks behind the curtain, little sense amid the striking, legendary technique of what drives her.

Which is no doubt as she wants it. Since shedding the "Funny Lady" persona to be just a lady, Streisand has been even more The Voice than a transparent personality.

57

Barbra
the Actress

BIOGRAPHY OF BARBRA STREISAND
Paramount Pictures, 1970

*A*s a little girl, Barbra Streisand dreamed of fame and stardom. Whether smearing lipstick on her face, "toe" dancing through the apartment or imitating television commercials in the mirror, she wanted to perform. Becoming an actress preoccupied her, although she was an honor student at Erasmus Hall High School in Brooklyn, New York, graduating with a 93 average and a medal in Spanish.

Recalling her early days looking for that "big break" in show business, she says, "It was degrading. No one should have to beg for a job. Demoralizing, totally demoralizing. They wouldn't audition you or even talk to you. I knew I was good. I made up my mind they'd have to come to me. 'Wait and see,' I vowed. 'I'll do it on my own.'"

Which is exactly what she did. Amateur night led to a night club booking at the Bon Soir in New York. Agents and producers dropped by to see and hear her but she insisted she was not a singer, but "an actress who sings." Without ever taking a singing lesson, the "actress who sings" found herself a very-much-in-demand singer.

Miss Streisand decided very early in life that she had "to be somebody." As she tells it, "I decided I didn't want to be just the best of one thing. I would be the best recording star, best Broadway star and best movie star."

As it turned out, Miss Streisand, who portrays a clairvoyant in Paramount Pictures' "On a Clear Day You Can See Forever," made good on her prophecies and her childhood ambitions all have come to pass. In 1962, Miss Streisand won the New York Drama Critics Award as Best Supporting Actress for her comic role as Miss Marmelstein in "I Can Get It For You Wholesale." In 1963, Cue Magazine honored her as its "Entertainer of the Year," an award she again won in 1970. The National Academy of Recording Arts and Sciences awarded her a Grammy as best solo female vocalist in 1963, 1964 and 1965. She won an Emmy Award for her television special, "My Name is Barbra" in 1965 and in 1969 she won the Academy Award as Best Actress of the Year for her portrayal of Fanny Brice in "Funny Girl." In 1970 she was presented with a Tony Award naming her "Star of the Decade." In addition, her role as Dolly Levi in the film version of "Hello, Dolly!" won critical acclaim.

Miss Streisand made it on her own terms. Her phenomenal progress in show business stems from an unlikely combination of qualities: she refers to herself as "lazy," but spends endless hours striving for the best, she is intuitive, she is a nonconformist, she is uncertain and yet determined. Most of all, she is an extremely talented young lady.

The highly individualistic Streisand taste in clothes has been reinterpreted in a manner befitting Barbra's two-time election to the International Best Dressed list. She made her singing debut clad in a plain black dress adorned with a now-popular antique vest and was way ahead of her time in fashion. She designed her own gowns, usually for lack of funds, and achieved an original look by forsaking satins and beads for gowns of cotton and men's suit fabric, the forerunner of today's young look.

FILM CREDITS
"Funny Girl"
"The Owl and the Pussycat"
"Hello, Dolly!"
"On a Clear Day You Can See Forever"—Paramount Pictures

THEATRE CREDITS
"Another Evening with Harry Stoones"—1961
"I Can Get It For You Wholesale"—1962
"Funny Girl"—1964–1965
"Funny Girl" (London)—1966

ALBUM RELEASES
"The Barbra Streisand Album"
"The Second Barbra Streisand Album"
"Barbra Streisand/The Third Album"
"People"

"My Name Is Barbra"
"My Name Is Barbra, Too"
"Color Me Barbra"
"Je M'Appelle Barbra"
"Simply Streisand"
"A Happening In Central Park"
"What About Today?"
"Barbra Streisand's Greatest Hits"
"I Can Get It For You Wholesale" (Original Cast Album)
"Pins and Needles" (Original Cast Album)
"Funny Girl" (Original Cast Album)
"Funny Girl" (Soundtrack Album)
"Hello, Dolly!" (Soundtrack Album)
"On a Clear Day You Can See Forever" (Soundtrack Album)

TELEVISION SPECIALS
"My Name Is Barbra"—1965
"Color Me Barbra"—1966
"Belle of 14th Street"—1967
"A Happening In Central Park"—1968

"*H*er face, alone, without trappings to distract from it or clothes to categorize it, was really quite lovely. Classic proportions, in general, the only flaw being a bit of teenage acne, which gave her a vulnerable, young look. Her nose wasn't as pronounced as it would seem to be, as the camera emphasizes it. I cannot, and could not, understand the criticisms from certain quarters about her being homely. I've worked with unattractive appealing actresses, and actors who were homely, or plain, or even ugly. Barbra had no ugliness about her. She could be made plain, without her Cleopatra eye make-up. It's a pity her marvelous waif quality hasn't been allowed to show through more."

—designer SIR CECIL BEATON

BARBRA STREISAND TALKS ABOUT HER "MILLION-DOLLAR BABY"

Gloria Steinem

Ladies' Home Journal, August 1966

"*T*his pregnancy is like a God-given thing," said Barbra, "and the timing couldn't have been better. I was beginning to feel like a slave to a schedule. Pretty soon I'll have nothing to do but cook and be pregnant five whole months. I can't wait!"

She would have earned more than a million dollars merely from one concert tour that has now had to be drastically curtailed, and the temptation was too much: Everybody immediately talked about a Million-Dollar Baby. "*Why* do they say that?" asked Barbra. "I mean, why must they measure everything in money? The most important thing is not what got canceled but that a healthy baby is born.

"I always thought that having babies was for other people," she went on, "but not for me." We were having tea before her evening's performance of *Funny Girl* in London, and the local critics—like those of every city she has ever appeared in—had just received her with raves that might have been written for Frank Sinatra and Sarah Bernhardt combined. But the time she spoke of was not the triumphant, star-spangled Now. (A very short Now at that: from a $50-a-week obscurity to multimillion-dollar status as, to quote a critic, "a living legend," took just five of her 24 years.) It was the homely, awkward, often anguished time of her growing up—a very lonesome Then.

"I was kind of a loner," she explained, "a real ugly kid. The kind who looks ridiculous with a ribbon in her hair. And skinny. My mother wouldn't let me take dancing lessons because she was afraid my bones would break; she was always shipping me off to some health camp. I would try to imagine my future, like other kids, but I couldn't, it just stopped. There was a big blank screen, no husband, no children, nothing. I decided that meant I was going to die—I wasn't being melodramatic or anything, I really believed it, and I would think, 'That's too bad, because I really could have done things.' "

Is it strange to think that her child will have a life so different from her own lower-middle-class one in Brooklyn? "Well," she smiled, "I can't suddenly get poor for her, or him, can I? But I don't want a child who has nothing but toys from F. A. O. Schwarz. Kids like simple things to play with: a piece of paper, a walnut shell. They should be dirty and basic when they want to be. I don't want to make her a kid brought up by the book. I think that if I can give her confidence and love and the feeling that she's wanted I'll be able to be honest, too; a person as well as a parent.

"That's the most important thing; that she feels loved and has *both* parents." Barbra's own father, a teacher of English and psychology, died of a cerebral hemorrhage when she was 15 months old and her brother, Sheldon, was nine. She looked thoughtful, as if remembering the years when her mother worked as a bookkeeper to support two children, and Barbra's bed was also the living-room couch. Friends say that she often asks questions about the father whom she doesn't remember, that she is proud of his promising career as an educator, and feels that her own life would have been different, not lonely, had he lived.

"That's the greatest thing about having a baby," she said, smiling again. "I get so self-involved, too focused on my own problems. But when I think of what's growing inside me, it's a miracle, the height of creativity for any woman. I used to dream about having a child, but it just didn't seem possible that it could happen to me; it seemed completely foreign. I even thought about adopting one. And now here I am and it's all going on in there. In December there will be a whole new human being.

"I've been reading medical books—I've always been fascinated by the way our bodies work: I'm not squeamish about it, or upset by the sight of blood—and it's incredible how it all functions. Each organ has a duty in the process, each part of it set off by complex signals . . . I'm telling you, it's not to be believed. There *must* be a God!"

Natural childbirth is definitely part of her plan. Both she and her husband, Elliot Gould, will go to classes in New York this fall. Barbra has already read a book by the Englishman Dr. Grantly Dick-Read, who pioneered the natural-childbirth movement.

"I can't understand how some women can just say, 'Give me an injection, I don't want to know a thing about it.' I mean, I really wonder about people like that. How can they miss the experience of birth? If they really feel it's some awful thing just to be got over, why do it at all?

"All those stories about how we'd been trying to have a baby for years were ridiculous. If we'd wanted a baby, we probably would have had one. I really think there's something mystical about conception. I mean, there are all those women who can't have children, adopt one, and then have one of their own because they relaxed about it. I'm sure there were many times when I could have got pregnant and didn't because I really wasn't ready yet; I was tense. I was too young.

"At first, I was worried about morning sickness, but I feel fine. The one time I was sick, it turned out to be the flu. And, for the first time in my life, I don't have longings for strange food. Usually, I love to eat, but now I never feel hungry, I just suddenly feel *empty*, and then I know my system needs food. My only symptom is an excessive need to sleep."

She had an urge to knit in the first weeks, which has now passed, leaving her with an unfinished baby blanket of orange, wine and pink. Her dresser is knitting on it while Barbra is onstage.

As for the name problem, that is nearly solved. "If it's a boy," said Barbra, "we'll probably call him Jason Emanuel: Jason just because we like it, and Emanuel because it was my father's name. For a girl, we're thinking of Samantha. It can change to suit her personality: Sam if she's adorable and kooky, Emmie if she's more sweet and serious, or the whole thing, Samantha, if she's exotic."

Elliot—"Elly," as Barbra calls him—was in New York on business that day, but would be back in a few days. The courtship which began when he was the talented, 23-year-old star of *I Can Get It For You Wholesale* and Barbra was a 19-year-old novice, has become one of the world's best-publicized marriages. That it has survived the strains of two careers and Barbra's streak to stardom is a tribute to them both. ("He handles it all very, very well," said Jerome Robbins, director of *Funny Girl*. "Elliot is a gentleman.") "To say I love Barbra," Elliot once told a reporter, "that's obvious. Otherwise I couldn't have stood it. I know the traps, I know the wounds, and I've decided it's worth it to wage the battle. People say theatrical marriages don't work. Our battle is especially difficult because we're real people, not just two profiles, two beautiful magazine covers. We really love one another."

Since they met, Elliot and Barbra have been together most of the time ("like Hansel and Gretel," as Barbra once explained) in the face of considerable professional pressures to keep them apart; probably he was the first person to really understand her, to stamp his image on the blank screen that she had seen as her future. ("She's fragile and exquisite," Elliot explained, "she needs taking care of. She liked me, and I think I was the first person who liked her back.") But scurrying back and forth between television shows, concerts, and movies, and all their separate commitments is not easy. They see the baby as something that will give them roots again.

Barbra's sense of differentness was always part misery, part confidence in her ability to "do things," but, looking at her in an English drawing room, sleekly coiffed and a deserving member of the Best-Dressed List, it was hard to remember that her early suffering had centered around the way she looked. In a world of snub-nosed American cheerleaders, she was clearly a misfit. She daydreamed, went to the movies and imagined herself on the screen, locked herself in the bathroom to carry on experiments with wild hair styles and dark lipstick ("I liked Rita Hayworth," she remembers. "I thought actresses had to be vampy"), and tried to fit into the pretty-girl ideal with "pink and white dresses with ruffles and lace—things I never should have worn."

At 14, she was an honor student at Erasmus High School in Brooklyn, a girl who never went to proms or had a date for New Year's Eve, but she had also made a friend. "One day I met this girl named Susan," she said, "who wore white makeup and kooky clothes. I liked her immediately." Susan helped to get her out of ruffles and free her sense of style ("I didn't sulk because I wasn't gorgeous," said Barbra, "I dressed wild to show I didn't care"), and, two years later, after graduating from high school, she left Brooklyn and any desire to be "ordinary, pretty like Shirley Temple," behind forever.

Still, even by Manhattan standards, she was a secret and very special girl. A member of an acting class that she attended briefly (between unsuccessful rounds of producers' offices and such part-time jobs as sweeping up at an off-Broadway theater) has a vivid picture of her as "always late,

69

very intense, wearing a coat of some immense plaid, and eating yogurt." Even her few close friends had no idea that she could sing until she got her now-famous $50-a-week job at a Village nightclub. Singing had been another part of her differentness, her private world, something she did alone on the roof of her New York apartment house, or sitting on the front steps on summer evenings. In fact, even the singing job seemed a compromise. She wanted to be an actress. "I knew I was good," she said stubbornly, "but no one would let me read till I had experience, so how could I get experience? Besides, I wasn't the ingenue type those casting creeps were looking for. I could have changed the way I looked, had my nose fixed or something, but I just wouldn't. That wouldn't have been honest, right?"

Finally, singing in a nightclub, her unique looks and style and talent began to pay off. In a middy blouse, shoes with enormous buckles, and neo-Cleopatra eye makeup, she sang such off-beat songs as "Who's Afraid of the Big Bad Wolf" and "Happy Days Are Here Again"—hardly the "No Business Like Show Business" medley of most young singers. Without a lesson to her name, she surprised everyone with her instinctive musicianship, a sense of gesture enhanced by attenuated, elegant hands, a gift for making any song into a three-act play, and a voice that was reminiscent of many great singers (Judy Garland, Lena Horne, Morgana King) while remaining special, and imitative of none. "I couldn't really have imitated anybody," explained Barbra, "because I hadn't really *heard* anybody. I'd never been to a nightclub until I worked in one."

The awkwardness, the price of being different didn't really stop there, but—as she went from the Village club to the Blue Angel, and from there to a show-stopping song in the Broadway musical *I Can Get It For You Wholesale*—she was compared to Nefertiti as often as "an amateur anteater" and to Cleopatra instead of a ferret. Slowly, she was breaking the cheerleader prototype of beauty and originating her own. By the time she had made several best-selling records, appeared on national television shows, and burst on New York as the star of *Funny Girl*, fashion magazines were announcing her as "the girl of the 'Sixties . . . a unique beauty . . . a superstar." All her *outré* habits of dress and makeup were enshrined as chic, and columnists wrote tributes to her "slender arabesque of neck" as well as to her talent.

Different. Different as a star. Different when she was finding her way. Different as a girl, raised in an Orthodox Jewish home. The latter she remembers as an archaic place with little to do with the real world. ("We couldn't cross our fingers, and we weren't allowed to say 'Christmas.' So as soon as the rabbi went out of the room, I would close my eyes, cross my fingers, and say 'Christmas, Christmas, Christmas' as much as I could.") But she does intend to teach her child about God. "I believe in God. The Orthodox training is outdated, but I think it's an unfair burden to teach a kid nothing; to say, 'I don't know, decide for yourself.' Science isn't everything. No one is ever going to come up with a scientific reason for dying. Organized religion is something I couldn't subscribe to, but it's important that we have a sense of God, a sense of mystery."

But the childhood sense of doom was with her then. ("I still thought I had some mysterious disease, and only two months to live. You really appreciate life," she added soberly, "when you think you're going to die.") And, sometimes, it still is. Each time she gets on a plane, she envisions what would happen, which people would say what if she were to die. After taping her last CBS television special, she flew to Paris, thinking all the way how sad it would be when the TV special was shown and she wasn't there. It happens less and less as she is more and more secure: the screen isn't empty now, and she can see ahead.

It isn't a question of exchanging a career for motherhood. Barbra will go on making records, films (the film version of *Funny Girl* will begin early in 1967) and television shows. The one medium she has ruled out is the stage: no more Broadway musicals, or any plays unless they are short runs in repertory. ("I'd love to play *Romeo and Juliet*, but I don't want to be saying the same words every night for years.") The baby will change her life in a deeper, more final way, because it is her link with humanity, her symbol of belonging at last. For a girl who never felt related to her own family ("I used to say, 'OK, Ma, did you find me on a doorstep or what?'"), to her friends or to her neighborhood ("Brooklyn," she says firmly, "was always someplace to get out of"), having a baby seems to be the most real proof of sameness, of relation to others, of continuity, of belonging.

If her child is a girl, would she like her to look the same, to have the painful specialness of talent?

71

Barbra is silent for a while. "I know that my childhood, everything I went through, is important to me, to art. It doesn't matter how she looks; she will be partly Elliot and partly me, but still herself. But I don't think I'd like to watch her go through exactly the same thing; no. Art isn't everything. Love is more important."

But, should her daughter be the exact image of Barbra, she would no longer be thought homely. Barbra Streisand has changed the bland, pug-nosed American ideal, probably forever. "She looks just like her mother," everyone would say. "She's beautiful."

BARBRA THE GREAT: TALENTED GIRL
ON A TRIUMPHAL MARCH

Pete Hamill

Cosmopolitan, February 1968

Records, TV, the Broadway stage . . . all these worlds have fallen before Barbra Streisand's talent. Now she's out in Hollywood.

*T*he movie at the front of the cabin was *Our Man Flint,* all about girls in purple bikinis saving the world from a mad scientist. I sat watching it at 35,000 feet, with a headset plugged into my skull, wondering vaguely about the smashing blonde beside me, and falling into a half doze. I dreamed of the Last Judgment: of great, turret-breasted women with lilac eyes and plaster-white teeth, rounding up the last surviving men in America. They had us in a vast grassy pen that somehow resembled the ball park of the Los Angeles Dodgers, and we stood there in the bright California sun, waiting for the final destruction. It was rumored that we were to be dropped over the edge of the Pacific Palisades, ten at a time, and in my dream the Amazons were all laughing, while a high, pure voice soared out over an invisible loudspeaker. Suddenly I realized the voice belonged to Barbra Streisand.

"People,

People who need people . . ."

"Do you brug in the brindirig?" the blonde said.

"What?" I shouted, awake now.

"Do blue dirk in the birmarring?" she said again. She had brilliant blonde hair and brown eyes and she was bursting out of her seat belt. I took off the headset.

"Do you work in the industry?" she said. Oh. She was not talking code. The industry was Hollywood: TV and movies and press agentry and talent selling. "No," I said. "I'm not part of the industry. I'm a reporter."

"Oh," she said. "I saw you reading all those clippings. I thought you must be in the industry."

Well, in a way, I would be writing about the industry, I explained. I was on my way to the Coast to write about Barbra Streisand.

"God," the smashing blonde said. "Isn't she beautiful? So exotic. And so . . . *talented.*"

And the girl started to tell me about her life. She was from Pennsylvania (not a deserted mining town, but almost), and she had started acting in high school and won a couple of beauty contests and then been married to a sergeant in the Air Force and then decided that she didn't want that kind of life ("tough steaks and puking children") and decided to go into show business. A year before she had gone west and was given a screen test and signed with an agent ("he's a bastard") and obtained a divorce and had been in two TV series so far ("small things, really, but you need the credits to get anywhere in the industry") and was studying at a dramatics school in West Hollywood. Somewhere over Idaho, she asked me if I knew Barbra Streisand well.

"Just slightly," I said. It was true.

Four years before, I had followed Barbra around for a few days, writing about her for the first time. She was a charming, funny girl then, with a zany stream of talk, a fine tough Brooklyn sense of the absurd, and, of course, the hard core of that beautiful talent. Everyone then talked about how her future was unlimited. She couldn't miss. And she didn't. In four years she had done everything a show-business talent could do, and a little more. She had made the covers of *Time* and *Vogue,* she had carried an entire Broadway show *(Funny Girl),* her record albums were big sellers. She had done two highly praised TV specials. She had given an outdoor concert in Central Park in New York, which brought out 130,000 people to hear her, while another 30,000 milled about on the edge of the park. She had married and, so far, it had lasted (although, in early December her husband, actor Elliot Gould, was bitterly complaining about Barbra's "dates" with Omar Sharif), and when she gave birth to a son, the New York *Daily News* threw all the affairs of the earth off the front page and went with a headline that said "MILLION DOLLAR BABY!"

Now she had come to Hollywood, to make a $10,000,000 film of her show, *Funny Girl,* a musical about Fanny Brice, and people in New York were wondering who would make the inevitable movie about Barbra Streisand.

"Tell me," the blonde said, "what's Barbra Streisand really like?"

I laughed out loud. The blonde was puzzled. "Sorry," I said. "I was just thinking of something." The blonde started reading *Variety* furiously. I slid low in the seat, stretching my legs. What is Barbra Streisand really like? What, indeed, is Claudia Cardinale really like, or John Wayne, or Brigitte Bardot? What, after all, is Lyndon Johnson really like? It was a joke: if we had learned anything in growing up, it was that we knew nothing about anyone and pretended that we did. I stretched again, my legs cramped from the journey. Then I heard something tear. The seat had gone out of my trousers. A long, deep slash, beyond emergency repair. I started laughing again. In the movies, Cary Grant would be the reporter and would take the blonde away with him for champagne and dancing and breakfast in bed. In real life, you sat with your pants split and your drawers showing, laughing blackly, wondering whether you would walk through the terminal with the typewriter or the briefcase behind you.

"Good luck with your story," the blonde said as we waited in the crowded aisle after landing. "Thanks," I said. "Good luck to you." She was looking at me as if I were really Richard Speck.

75

I was met by a girl named Carol Shapiro from the Columbia Pictures publicity office. Yes, Barbra was fantastic. She had such talent. She was marvelous so far in *Funny Girl*. It was too bad I hadn't been on the set a few days before when she had done a ballet.

"I studied dancing," Miss Shapiro said, "and all I can say is that Barbra must have studied dancing, too, at some point. Nobody could have that kind of grace and poise without studying somewhere along the line."

"Maybe it's just California," I said. "Maybe it's just that out here you can do anything."

"No," Miss Shapiro said. "It's talent."

I checked into the Beverly Hills Hotel, one of the great hotels in this country. Miss Shapiro telephoned Jack Brodsky, the unit publicity man, who said he would send a car for me in the morning. She gave me a handful of press releases and we said good night in my room. I sent the trousers to the valet for repair, and then called an old friend, Budd Schulberg [author of *What Makes Sammy Run?* and *The Disenchanted*]. He lives in Beverly Hills, not far from the hotel. I went up to see him, in a cab. He was in his second year as director of a writing workshop in the strange, bleak, Negro ghetto of Watts. His son was in Vietnam.

That night, we drank whiskey and talked until almost five o'clock in the morning.

Miss Shapiro and I drove out to the studio at 10:15. Usually, the day in the industry starts at 8 A.M., and sometimes earlier. William Wyler, the director of *Funny Girl,* had worked out a different schedule. He preferred European hours—a day that started at 11 A.M. and went to about 7 P.M.— because his stars could then have some social life in the evenings, and still be fresh and relaxed in the morning.

We parked in the anonymous black-topped Columbia Pictures parking lot, where the rank and file keep their cars, and walked to the main entrance. *Funny Girl* was shooting in Studio 16. It was about three city blocks away from the entrance, and the life of the movie lot seemed busy and full. A large Negro sold cigarettes and cigars and Cokes from a stand: carpenters and stage hands hammered and sawed in a workshop. In front of Studio 16, four horses munched on a pile of hay—living props for a Gregory Peck Western being shot around the corner. In the Studio 16 private parking lot, there were cars in the space reserved for Ray Stark, producer of *Funny Girl,* and William Wyler, the director. Barbra Streisand's space was still empty. The door was locked on the trailer that served as her dressing room, and the golf cart used for transporting her around the lot was parked out front.

Inside Studio 16, the vast resources of the Hollywood technicians had assembled a detailed replica of an 1890s Coney Island dance hall and beer garden: a huge proscenium and an orchestra pit with a runway wrapped around it, two tiers of balconies at left and right, old electric fans hanging from the ceilings, the whole place decorated with gold scrollwork, paintings of Greek maids and sylvan gardens, all art nouveau and innocence, like the 1890s themselves.

"Where's Barbra?" I asked.

"Oh, she'll be along soon," Miss Shapiro said. "You should have a good day. They're doing the dance on roller skates today."

While carpenters hammered, electricians fiddled with lights, and men complaining of hangovers gulped paper cup after paper cup of cold water from the cooler, I read the movie script. *Funny Girl* is all about a fictional character named Fanny Brice. There was a real Fanny Brice, of course, but hardly any of the people who go to movies these days can remember her, and those who do think of her as Baby Snooks, a radio character of the thirties and forties.

In the script, she is a homely girl who makes good through art. The saga goes like this: Fanny tries out for a show in this Coney Island dance hall. She is So Bad, She's Funny. The audience gives her a Standing Ovation. The people who run the dance hall have no foresight. They don't know what they Have. They Throw Her Out. She sings a lament. The World Is a Desolate Place. But wait. Ziggy was Out Front. The great Ziegfeld, who was Out Front in every show-biz saga in the history of man. He was Out Front for Jolson. He was Out Front for the Dolly Sisters. He was even Out Front for John Payne. Now, he is Out Front for Fanny Brice. He comes back, signs her for the Follies, and, overnight, Fanny is A Star. But wait. Into every show-biz life Some Rain Must Fall. In Fanny Brice's life, the Rain is Nicky Arnstein. Nicky is the blight of her life, her only real tragedy. He is a gambler. They have a romance, they marry. He Treats Her Badly. She Walks Out. He Wants Her back. She Won't Take Him. She must live with this personal tragedy. She is Laughing on the Outside, Crying on the Inside. Fade-out.

Ah, well. *Funny Girl* worked on Broadway. Maybe the movie would work. Columbia and Ray Stark were betting $10,000,000 that it would and, besides, since *The Sound of Music*, musicals were respectable again; they had been Out for a long time; now the Sound of Money had brought them back. I was finishing the script when Barbra Streisand arrived.

She was dressed in a maroon jumper with a sailor neck, baggy, black, little girl knickers, black high-button shoes. And she was talking to Ray Stark. Stark is a friendly, medium-sized man with red hair, a face pink from the sun, who worries a lot about his weight, and is, in many ways, the antithesis of a conventional Hollywood producer. I never heard him call anyone baby, he respects experimental film makers, and he can entertain you with good talk about painters, writers or sculptors while carrying the grosses of his pictures in his head. He was also Fanny Brice's son-in-law, and the original Broadway show and now the movie was his idea. Streisand seemed taller than he was (because of the heels), and they talked intensely for a few minutes. Stark saw me, remembered me from a brief meeting in Montego Bay a few years before, said hello.

Barbra said, "How are you?" A woman in a blue smock was standing behind her, studying the costume. She suddenly noticed a small scuff on the heel of Barbra's right shoe. She moved off swiftly. Stark took Barbra on the side for a brief talk. The woman in the blue smock came back with an aerosol can in her hand and without saying a word, knelt down and sprayed Barbra's black shoe.

"Goddammit," the woman said, looking at the can. "It's *brown*!"

Barbra looked down and shrugged, said good-bye to Stark, and started toward the stage. "How has it been so far, making your first film?" She smiled. The gray eyes lit up.

"It's—well, half fun and half—you know."

She made a trembling gesture with her hands.

All movie sound stages have their own peculiar life and their own peculiar sense of time. Strangers are thrown together for weeks, months, hours; their money, talent, time, drives, egos, ambitions, failures, and fears are mobilized towards this one thing: the production and completion of a motion picture. The visiting journalist can seldom arrive at much truth; he is a voyeur, entering this strange world for a while and returning with fragments. He comes home, and writes his piece, and stands in a favorite saloon with friends, and someone asks, "What's she really like?"

"I don't know," you say. And nobody believes you. So you recite the fragments, because they are your only evidence. In Hollywood, in the days I was there, I didn't talk much to Barbra Streisand. In the four years since I first wrote about her, she had become a star. Not one of your ordinary, run-of-the-mill Donna Reed–Deborah Kerr–Peggy Lee–Sandra Dee stars. But a Superstar. I hadn't seen it happen; I was away a lot during those years, in other countries and on the road. I had seen one of the TV specials, a rather campy creation that had Barbra Streisand as a little girl playing in a department store at night, or something. It seemed pretentious and plummy, with a cloying, self-conscious air to it. It was the sort of faggy, aren't-we-cute thing that was very big in New York that season. But through it all there was Barbra's wonderful voice—eclectic in its ethnic range, yes, but full and rich, shimmering with drama and controlled passion. That voice was no mere mechanical instrument; it was a dramatic weapon, and she used it to its limits and a step beyond. These was, to be sure, something arch about the choice of songs: They were those special little songs that vanish from the mind the morning after you have seen the show, and enter the repertoire of piano players in intimate saloons. Yet, even these became something as Barbra polished and burnished them with that voice.

In Hollywood, there was another influence at work. Barbra Streisand had become such a big star, had gone through such a flawless four years, that she had already entered into the peculiar isolation of fame. Miss Shapiro and Jack Brodsky, the publicity people, tried to get her to sit down with me to talk, but Barbra was busy with work, or studying the script, or having her baby over at lunch time, or talking to Wyler.

It didn't matter to me and, of course, it didn't matter to her. And yet there was something oddly pathetic about it all: When Barbra Streisand wanted to sit down, someone was there with the chair. When she sat down, makeup people surrounded her, patting the dampness of her face, straightening a loose hair, checking the shoes, handing her a script—*Yes, Miss Streisand . . . No, Miss Streisand . . . Of course, Miss Streisand.* The terrible thing to me was that she had grown used to it. She was Barbra Streisand the Superstar now, and she didn't need anybody. She could be rude to people if she chose to (and she was, possibly unconsciously), and she could be pleasant. It didn't matter.

What did matter was keeping her winning streak going. So far, she had done everything right. Now, it was apparent she felt the film version of *Funny Girl* had to be her *greatest* triumph.

So she would go through a scene over and over until it was precisely right. Wyler had never directed a musical before, and was sharing the direction of the film with a tall, lean man named Herb Ross. Ross was directing all the musical scenes, with Wyler looking on.

I watched Barbra go through take after take of some scenes. Occasionally, Ross would finish, say the scene was fine, please print it, and want to move on, and then Barbra would have an idea, some minor alteration, and they would go through it again and she would be *right* and the scene would be marvelous. Other times, she was just moving a simple scene into a more baroque version, adding scrollwork and curlicues as tormented as the art work on the pasteboard walls of the reconstructed dance hall. Producer Ray Stark would look in once in a while, knowing the production was behind schedule, hoping it would catch up. No, he told me, there had never been any question that anyone but Barbra would play the lead in the *Funny Girl* film version.

"Barbra is good," Stark said. "With Willy Wyler, she's great. When she was a success in the play, there was no question about who would do the movie. I just felt she was too much a part of Fanny, and Fanny was too much a part of Barbra to have to give it to someone else. Sure, there's always an element of risk when you take someone who has never made a film and put her in a $10,000,000 production. But this is *Barbra Streisand*. Plus Willie Wyler. Plus Herb Ross. Willie Wyler has had thirteen Academy Award nominations. He has won three Academy Awards." Wyler, a small white-haired man who smokes long filter-tip cigarettes and has a kind face, said: "Barbra can do anything. We haven't asked her to do anything that she can't do. And she does it half a dozen different ways and that makes my job easier. She's not the most relaxed person, but neither am I. She worries about everything. I think that's fine. Lots of people don't worry about anything, but I'd rather have her worry about too much than too little."

Watching Barbra work, you can see how the *Funny Girl* movie might become something really first class. One afternoon, I was reading the call sheet. There were 138 extras sitting in the audience in bowler hats and mustaches and bustles; 12 musicians in the pit; 10 show girls from the chorus line, dancing marvelously on roller skates; 4 assistant directors; 18 lamp operators; 11 hairdressers; 15 costumers; 9 men working on the cameras; 7 prop men; 8 grips [scene shifters]; 2 still photographers; and 1 cop, standing at the door. Barbra was sitting in her canvas chair between takes, talking in her scattering, rapid voice.

"It was never true that I had no discipline," she was saying. "It's just that I *never* played to the balcony. I always played to the best seat in the theater. I always played to my own reality." Fanny Brice was important to her. "She was very much like myself," Barbra said. Then Stark arrived and she left with him, breaking off our talk without a word.

Soon, she was up on the stage, playing a clumsy, knock-kneed young girl, moving with a peculiar kind of awkward grace. In the script, this was the moment after Fanny's fiasco in the dance hall. Now, Barbra was singing to the audience, alone on the stage. The song was "Am I Blue?" The young girl was tentative at first, not sure of a reception, but then the audience was with her, the music building, the voice subtly moving from hesitation to full confidence and then rolling onto a rousing finale. It was an exacting and artful performance, and even the grips and stagehands— the most hardened men in Hollywood—broke into applause. For the first time I understood what she was doing with this very ordinary script. She was treating it the way a great performer treats an old standard. She was looking deeply into it, past the glib surface, and locating the emotion that was there at the start, before repetition and second-rate artists had corrupted it. She did almost a dozen takes of the scene, and each time it came out fresh. The hired audience of extras was dazzled. So was I. At the end of the day, after the dance number, Barbra took off her roller skates and walked across the sound stage in slippers.

"I was trying to decide how to describe my life to you," she said. "All these people patting you, and talking to you, and working you over. It's like being a fighter. A fighter between rounds."

She went into the trailer, while the extras lined up at the telephone down the studio street to call the casting office about other jobs.

A number of people I talked to that week said that Barbra Streisand was a peculiar sort of girl to be in Hollywood as a Superstar, in her first film. There was, first of all, the matter of her looks. You could feel something in all those hordes of extras that was the spirit of malice and resentment. There were a lot of women in their forties, who once had traveled west like the blonde on the plane. They had had the teeth capped and the nose fixed but, somehow, nothing had happened. They had blamed it on

81

agents, or luck, or not sleeping with the right people, and one morning the creamy flesh was wrinkling and they knew that none of it would happen and they were working on the Strip or as extras in other people's movies. They would never really understand Barbra Streisand. Her sculptured, Semitic nose; everybody has written about it and talked about it. But instead of hurting her, Barbra Streisand's nose was now part of her beauty, turning her into an exotic. The looks and the voice made her an *original*. Both of those plus the work.

One morning I dropped by her rented house in Beverly Hills. There were three automobiles in the driveway and a small dog named "Sadie" running around the house, and a lawn sprinkler turned lazily outside. I had coffee, Barbra came down with her husband, a good-looking young man named Elliot Gould, who was dressed in corduroys and had his hair grown long for a part in a film called *The Night They Raided Minsky's*. Barbra was late. She said good-bye to Gould and we dashed to the car. She slid behind the wheel, turned around, and was about to leave when her hairdresser, a middle-aged Negro named Grace Davidson, rushed out, followed by the dog. She got into the back seat of the car with the dog. Barbra talked all the way as we drove through the seedy center of Hollywood.

"A performer has a given task," she said. "It's part of the job to do it right. You don't ask the motivation. You just do it . . . I'm very tight with my time. It's a tough fight to get me to do interviews. I have too much to do and think about. If you talk or verbalize too much about your inner feelings, then your feelings don't mean the same thing they once did. Then reporters get your meaning wrong, anyway. It's very frustrating.

"Almost since the beginning, all the publicity has been frustrating. The stories are always so stupid. There's one going around now that, because the new photographs of me look good, I must have had my nose done. They can't just say that I look good and forget about it. That's one reason why I couldn't care less about publicity."

Did she ever stop working? Was there anything done for enjoyment, when she was not thinking about her work and the film and what she would do the next day?

"No, never," she said, driving easily, enjoying the feel of the huge car, a Chrysler Imperial, as it moved through the hot streets. "I guess that's hard on the people who live with me. But I can't . . ."

* * *

There were other things happening in the world—she realized that; yet these things were often too depressing to think about. "Our foreign policy is very—unreal. I guess they think they are sticking to the American tradition or something. But all that waste and killing. Maybe we just will have to learn to lose some face. I mean, this is the destruction of the earth we're risking. In a way, it's probably all inevitable. The thing is that, so far, any scientific development exceeds our emotional development. Our leaders sometimes seem very childish. They don't seem to realize that we can destroy ourselves."

She was quiet for a moment.

"That's one reason why I decided I was not going to waste my time on trivia," she said. "Life is too short and precarious. The hippies are going the other way. They're looking for some kind of instant Nirvana on drugs. But you can never give up fighting. That's the thing. I feel I've got to take advantage of my time. Life is too important to put up with a lot of silly things."

The solution was work. Barbra said working on a movie with Ross and Wyler was one of the important things.

"We can disagree on a point of interpretation," she said. "But money is being spent; you've got to *do* something. You've got to produce. There's no time for self-indulgence."

Movies, she said, were "a different kind of discipline from the theater. All those bright lights, close to the retina, lots of people standing around . . . you can't fake anything. That camera sees too clearly." She wondered about success, and what had happened to her, and all the people out there in the audience who didn't know anything about her at all, except that she was an entertainer.

"If I *had* something to say to them," she said, "I would say, 'Don't envy.' Everybody in their own way has problems. They should try to make their own lives the fullest they can be."

Throughout her monologue, she was cool, almost cold. She had a day's work ahead of her. I asked her how she liked Hollywood and Los Angeles in general.

"Well, it doesn't matter where you live," Barbra said. "It's how you

83

live, what you live, who you live with. And the rest is extra. Like the weather. This is a small town, really, in its attitudes. It has its status symbols and its small, narrow life. But I'm not involved in any of that. I just appreciate the weather, and the driving. But the place doesn't really matter."

We were at the studio, and the gate was rising as the guard waved us in. Extras were moving toward Stage 16. Barbra Streisand got out and said good-bye and went off to see rushes. That was it. The girl from Brooklyn with the odd-looking face and the big talent was a star now, and there was nothing really to find out about her. I went to the press office to arrange for a ride to the hotel, where I could check out and get a plane back to New York. At the cigarette stand, I met one of the *Funny Girl* extras, a heavy-set woman with washed-out orange hair. She was seventy-eight years old and said she was once married to Fatty Arbuckle, the comedian of the silent era whose career was destroyed in a lurid sex scandal.

"Are you having fun?" she said.

"Sort of," I said.

"Barbra is a real star, isn't she?" she said, and her voice was sad and wistful with the knowledge of too many years spent in the industry, looking for jobs, and seeing all the bright young people arrive and blaze finely and vanish again. "She has a lot of talent."

"Yes, she does," I said.

At the airport, I picked up a paper. The front page was about a fierce battle in Vietnam, away out there in the real world, where real young men spilled real blood and fired real guns. There was an item in a gossip column saying that Barbra Streisand was being "difficult" on the set of *Funny Girl* and the production was far behind schedule. I didn't really care. All the way back to New York I slept without dreaming. And coming into the city, I thought about a young Negro soldier I had seen in Vietnam one afternoon in a place called Bong Son. One moment he was standing beside me. The next moment he was dead with a bullet slammed into his chest. I never found out if he had any talent.

HELLO, DOLLY!—THE 1890 MANHATTAN STAGE SET

20th Century Fox press release, 1969

*T*he set itself is the largest and most expensive—more than $2,000,000—ever attempted for a 20th Century–Fox picture, and perhaps for any other film. It is a complex of 60 buildings, involving reproductions of intersections of Manhattan's Fifth Avenue, Broadway and Mulberry Street, Madison Square Park, 14th Street and the Bowery.

If laid out in a straight line, the set would have stretched about three-fifths of a mile. Through it runs a six hundred foot reconstruction of the Sixth Avenue elevated railway with a working steam engine and three cars operated by a retired Union Pacific engineer.

If a multi-skilled worker started on the job in 1968, he would finish 119 years later!

Enough paint was used on the exterior sets alone to cover every house in a 5,000 population town; more than 10 tons of nails were used at the last count and the end wasn't in sight; 858,000 board feet of lumber were cut and fabricated. Just for the record, 858,000 board feet of lumber translates into 117 miles!

More than 330,000 square feet of plywood were used, enough to build all the houses in that mythical town of 5,000 population.

The Manhattan scene is also crowded with 22 miles of telephone and electric lines now carried underground. Alexander Graham Bell had demonstrated his invention in 1877, and the telephone was coming into its own in 1890. Electric power, too, was in general use in the city.

In an interesting coincidence, Edison demonstrated his Kinetoscope, called "the ancestor of all motion picture systems," on October 6, 1889. This was made possible by George Eastman's development of strips of film for his earliest Kodak, only a few months previously. Eastman's company also produces the film for *Hello, Dolly!*

All this formed a background for the most stupendous effort ever attempted by a film company in America—the parade sequence. A total of 675 persons were in the parade, passing through 3,108 extras. The nearest comparable statistic in 20th Century–Fox was the funeral of Queen Victoria in *Cavalcade,* which involved a total of 3,000 persons.

Perhaps the best idea of the size of the operation can be gained from the logistics that were behind it: Two soundstages and three circus tents were staffed with 122 make-up and wardrobe artists for the crowd. There were 15 special assistant directors, costumed so they could function within view of the four Todd-AO cameras. Thirty-five uniformed policemen directed traffic and five costumed detectives mingled in the crowd.

The 146 horses involved were trained beforehand not to be panicked by the music, as was the pig carried by actress Judy Knaiz on the Meat Packers Float. Schedules of three television series were changed so that they would not be shooting on the lot that week, and all regular employees not involved were urged to take their vacations then. Sixty watering stations, 17 special toilet facilities and five first aid stations were set up.

At its peak, the parade cost about $200,000 a day above and beyond the normal daily production costs of *Hello, Dolly!*

SUPERSTAR: THE STREISAND STORY
Joseph Morgenstern
Newsweek, January 5, 1970

*B*y any standard but raw musculature, Barbra Streisand is the most powerful entertainer in America today. She could get financing if she wanted her next movie to be based on Van Nostrand's Scientific Encyclopedia. (Not such a bad idea: we open on "Photosynthesis," with Barbra in the greenhouse dressed in silver lamé gardening togs . . .) She's seen on the screen in *Hello, Dolly!* in 70-mm Todd-AO, she's heard on records in 360 Stereo Sound, and she's dissected by gossip columnists in 8-point malice. The movie version of *Funny Girl*, her first star vehicle, which won her an Academy Award, is still playing on Times Square. *On a Clear Day You Can See Forever* will be released next spring, and she's now shooting *The Owl and the Pussycat* in New York.

Several of her TV specials have been stunning. Her records have sold nearly nine million copies. She seems to be seen everywhere, and the volume of copy is vast about what she does, where she goes and with whom. How she wields her personal power is one thing. How she uses her artistic power is another, though, and it is the essential thing about her, as it has been ever since she appeared on Broadway more than seven years ago as Miss Marmelstein in *I Can Get It For You Wholesale*. What matters most about her is her gifts, or her art, or whatever you want to call it. It's how she's able to make such a lot go such a long way.

She made her Miss Marmelstein entrance in a swivel chair: Yetta Tessye Marmelstein, a bizarre, beehived, unbeloved child of 19, swooping and swiveling towards us to ask why other girls get called by their first names right away. "Oh, *why* is it always Miss Marmelstein . . . ?" She chose that preposterous chairbound entrance because she was too scared to face her audience standing up and because most secretaries, she figured, spend most of their time in chairs anyway. A great performance is a collection of such precisely right choices: theatrical, extravagant, but above all true. She rolled on stage, and then the most peculiar thing happened. This beehive office girl who really seemed to have come out of an office put on a whole little musical by herself. It was heroic, in its way, and desperately funny.

Wallflower: The heroine that she so quickly became had a particular desperation all her own. She was a wallflower. She had this Jewish problem, and this homely problem. "Nobody Makes a Pass at Me," she sang in the 25th anniversary recording of *Pins and Needles,* a garment workers' union show with a charming score by Harold Rome, who also did the *Wholesale* score. It was much the same character that Rome had written in the Miss Marmelstein number, except that Barbra threw new anger into it, comic self-hate and harsh self-appraisal. "Just like Ivory soap, I'm 99 and 44/100ths percent pure," she wailed, and the "pure" came out as a filthy word. *PURE!*

She was purely her own invention, nothing prefabricated, no resemblance to starlets living or dead. She was a regular person with a genuine past from a real place that happened to be Brooklyn, which made people laugh. She really was pure, but pure what, exactly? Her first starring role, Fanny Brice in the Broadway production of *Funny Girl,* supplied one answer—pure oddball. It was such a persuasive answer that it seemed for a time to be the only one.

"When you're younger," she said slowly and cautiously in a long discussion of her work one recent evening, "you have only your imagination to draw on, so what happens is it transcends reality, it almost makes its own art." She was talking, at this point, about her work as an acting-school student of 16 or 17. (According to a friend who knew her then, she was the only one in the class who asked questions, who wasn't passive, wasn't awed by the teacher or the material.) "As you get older," Barbra said, "reality sets in."

Whatever its shortcomings as a cohesive piece of theatre, *Funny Girl* made remarkably shrewd use of its star. The choreography gave her a chance to do some sublime clowning in the "Beautiful Bride" number, in which Fanny, surrounded by long-stemmed beauties, sang sweetly that she was the beautiful reflection of her love's affection, which was all well and good except that girl was visibly, hugely pregnant. Isobel Lennart's book gave her an antic façade and a romantic, passionate spirit. The score, by Jule Styne and Bob Merrill, gave her two distinctive ballads—"People" and "The Music That Makes Me Dance." Most shrewdly of all, the score provided an opening number, sung not by Fanny but by her friends and neighbors, that briskly explored the problem of success, sex and the homely girl: "If a Girl Isn't Pretty" ("If a girl's incidentals aren't bigger than two lentils . . .")

In her own opening number she sang wistfully, comically, that she was the greatest star but no one knew it. By the time the movie version of *Funny Girl* came out in 1968 almost everyone knew it. Rather, they knew with more than a little skepticism that she was supposed to be the greatest. But Barbra had never made a movie, and cameras are notorious unmaskers of fraud. The cameras in *Funny Girl* unmasked an artist even more gifted than she was supposed to be. I remember worrying about superlatives in my review. Would I make a fool of myself by calling it the most accomplished, original and enjoyable musical comedy performance ever put on film? I searched my memory and finally decided that, what the hell, it simply was the greatest; why not say so?

Livepan: But what do such superlatives mean? What did she do that was so good? A fair question to ask and a hard one to answer, since the one thing she didn't do was hold still long enough for the categorizers to draw a clear bead on her. She did a livepan deadpan, a deadpan livepan. She had her ethnic material at least both ways, comedy and parody plus a bit of self-parody thrown in whenever she wanted to play dummy to her own ventriloquist. She worked a warm, romantic singing voice against a taut, comic speaking voice. Her transitions from one mood to the next were instantaneous and dazzling. In the scene leading to "Don't Rain on My Parade," she put her hands over her ears, shook her head and said "Don't tell me" as her fellow Follies girls tried to convince her that her man, Nicky Arnstein, was a stinker. Suddenly, without warning, she was into her song, repeating "Don't tell me" with an explosive "Don't" that carried her all the way to a tugboat deck and intermission.

Her energy was limitless, her sense of fun almost infallible. And at the end of a movie that didn't have its own dramatic end—poor pasteboard Nicky comes back to Fanny from the hoosegow but their marriage has nowhere to go—Barbra sang "My Man." She had the sound recorded live, an artistic gamble which most movie-stars wouldn't dream of taking. She wore black against a black background: nothing to be seen or heard of her but two hands, a face and a voice. She started small, injured, all trembly-tearful as if there were nothing else to do with an old chestnut about a lovelorn lady. Before the end of the first chorus, however, her funny girl made a decision to sing herself back to life. Her voice soared defiantly, a spirit lost and found in the space of a few bars, and since you paid your money you could now take your choice of being wiped out by the sheer, shameless sentiment of the situation, or by the virtuosity of an actress look-ing lovely, feminine and vulnerable at the same time she was belting out a ballad with the force of a mighty Wurlitzer.

We talked about typecasting. Italian audiences had no interest in seeing Marcello Mastroianni's superb performance in *The Organizer*. They wanted their romantic leading man, not a union organizer out of the smoky past. American audiences were indifferent to Cary Grant's fine work in Clifford Odets's film about an ill-starred Cockney, *None but the Lonely Heart*. "I suppose the audience just didn't buy it because they want what they un-derstand," Barbra said uncertainly, with no pleasure at the thought. "But . . . I can't buy that either. I always think if something's really good and right they've got to buy *that*. I mean I want to play all different kinds of parts: you know, from bitches to sweet girls to stupid girls to bright girls to every kind of girl. 'Cause I have all these possibilities. I'm slightly dumb, I'm very smart. I'm many things. You know? I want to use them, want to express them. It's kind of funny, because I'm in these sort of big pictures and yet I'm an odd . . . I'm an odd ball. I mean, I'm not a Doris Day or a Julie Andrews. That's what's weird about it. I don't know how I got into these things. Honestly."

She mistrusts the press but trusts the audience. "The audience is the best judge of anything. They cannot be lied to. I mean, this is something I discovered . . . not discovered . . . but after almost two years on the stage one learns that. The slightest tinge of falseness, they go back from you, they retreat. The truth brings them closer. A moment that lags, I mean, they're gonna cough. A moment that is held, they're not gonna cough. They don't know why, they can't intellectualize it, but they know it's right

91

or wrong. Individually they may be a bunch of asses but together as a whole they are the . . . wisest thing.''

Of all the gossip that's gossiped about her, the most intriguing part is her reputation for being difficult to work with. She has this habit, people say, of directing her directors. People often say that about stars. Power is a fascinating subject, and people love to think of moviemaking in terms of power, as an epic struggle between egomaniacs: on one side the director, wearing jodhpurs, boots, riding crop, monocle and leer; on the other side the star, fussing with her face and refusing to play her scene in the county workhouse unless they let her wear the Golden Fleece. One never knows the truth of these things. The actor-director relationship is uniquely intimate. One can only make guesses based on the movie's end result.

Her director in *Funny Girl* was William Wyler, a man of vast experience and proven artistry. He'd made some 40 movies before this; Barbra had made none. She, on the other hand, had created her own role, had played it 798 times on Broadway and in London and knew more about it, instinctively and intellectually, than anyone else on earth. There was every reason for these two artists with complementary equipment to collaborate on the film and—based on the strong end result—every reason to believe they did collaborate. Not without anger or pain, surely, since stars and directors are both playing for high stakes in such elaborate productions, but not without purpose either.

As a matter of fact, if Barbra directed Gene Kelly, her director in *Hello, Dolly!*, she should have done a better job. There's no evidence that he or anyone else directed this great, plodding dinosaur of a film. It's there because it's there, an impressive industrial enterprise in which everyone came dutifully to work in the mornings and picked up where they'd left off the day before. Kelly stages his turn-of-the-century comedy in late 1940s style, as if movie musicals stopped growing when he stopped dancing in them. Like Michael Kidd's choreography, Kelly's technique is antique at best, incompetent at worst. Several shakily written comedy scenes are just as shakily performed because no one knew how to direct or cut them. The *Hello, Dolly!* number comes in fits and starts because no one knew how to make it build, visually or dramatically. The 40 million extras in the big parade scene look like a routine rabble because no one knew where to put the cameras.

Fight: Like her co-stars—Walter Matthau as Horace, Michael Crawford as Cornelius—Barbra has an uphill fight with the foolish material and the flatfooted style. She needs help and doesn't get it, and it hurts. In search of a center for the character of Dolly Levi, she finds two, three or four centers and therefore none: Mae West, Vivien Leigh, Fanny Brice, even Barbra Streisand. She's too young for the part of this doughty Mrs. Fixit, so she does some of her best work out of character. Yet the movie dies utterly when she's off screen and comes obediently back to life when she's on. She may be in trouble from time to time but she bails herself out, and the movie as well, with great resourcefulness.

She spoofs the dumb material, or goes with it, or plays with it and against it almost simultaneously. "Such a long life line!" she cries in mock amazement as she reads Matthau's palm, then continues to read it like a hip gypsy. Leaving Matthau in the second act, she does another lightning transition from speech to song—"So Long Dearie"—with seven preposterously impassioned good-byes that she sings, trills, yodels and groans in the styles of Piaf, Marlene Dietrich and, for all I know, Lucrezia Borgia. Trapped by a scene in which Dolly teaches the waltz to an actor we know perfectly well is a professional dancer, she shows him the first rudimentary *one*-two-three, stands back while he does some exuberant look-ma-I'm-dancing adagios, and then cuts through the whole choice idiocy with a muttered ad lib: "I think he's been holding out on us."

As in *Funny Girl*, she does a parade number, "Before the Parade Passes By," for her first-act curtain. She's alone on the screen at first, a warm, throbbing body in coarse cartoon-land. Her Dolly is trying to gather her forces in this first chorus (force gathering is what first-act curtains are all about) so she can make her way back into the parade of life. Then there's a drum, and then an elephantine production number that takes the metaphor of the song literally: a parade with 76,000 trombones and the entire membership of the Screen Extras Guild. And the most amazing thing of all is that the parade itself, for all its blare and vulgar trappings, never comes up to the power of Barbra's performance in the first chorus, just as the whole "Hello, Dolly!" production number adds very little to the outland-

93

ish delight of her entrance, a middle-aged marriage broker being played by a sexy young woman in a sparkling gold gown. The girl is human, the production ain't. Who needs it?

That's an odd thing for an oddball to be taxed with, looking sexy and young. Was it done with mirrors, or with Irene Scharaff's costumes, or with Harry Stradling's photography? No, the suspicion doesn't withstand scrutiny because the girl does withstand it. She looks lovely on screen and off, so much so that you wonder what happened to her and when. Had she been taking ugly pills for the *Funny Girl* role and then quit cold turkey? The answer, of course, is that her publicity and her material in the first few years of her career told us she was an oddball, so an oddball is what we saw. She looked lovely in all but the most antic comedy routines of *Funny Girl*, yet the material kept saying Homely, Clumsy, Gawky, Screwy, so we took our cues. On records she was singing "Lover, Come Back to Me" with superbly dirty sexuality five years before *Funny Girl* hit the screen, and singing her slow, sensual versions of "Happy Days Are Here Again" and "Who's Afraid of the Big Bad Wolf" six months before that. The main and basic source of the confusion was that she'd started her Broadway career as a little old maid. Only later did she youthen.

What kind of actress is she? Where do her strengths lie? "Elliot [husband Elliot Gould] once took his great-grandmother to see me and she was about 85, and she said she liked me because I was so natural—so *natchel*. And I liked that. I guess my best attribute is my instinct. It just . . . it hurts me if I hear a wrong line reading or something. And there is no such thing as a wrong line reading, only there is. I mean, everything is so damned . . . needs to be qualified so." A line reading that didn't work, then? "Yeah. Right. It's like music. I mean, acting is even like music. Because I believe in rhythm, you know? Everything is dominated by our heartbeats, by our pulses, when one goes against certain rhythms it's jarring, it's unnatural, unless we use the dissonance."

She was squirming now and embarrassed by herself. "I'm not articulate and I'm not eloquent. This makes it sound like a lot of crap. It just sounds awful. I mean I hear it! But the point is I read a script and I hear and I see what the people are doing, and I'll have an idea right off the bat, and it's always my first instinct that I trust. I'm also very lazy so I don't delve much further."

When her first flop comes, what kind does she want it to be? "A big one," she grinned. "So I can have a good comeback."

What about other styles of acting? She didn't feel close to actors with "thought-out line readings—you know, they know exactly where the intonation goes, what the key word in the sentence is, what they're reaching for in their speech or whatever, I'm more moved when I see Brando, when I can't quite define his moments, when I see just *a* life, *a* mind, *a* personality. Brando is stronger than any of the characters he plays. There is a difference between preconceiving everything and having it in control, and when it's slightly out of control."

Mercurial: We talked about specific performances, agreeing on Jeanne Moreau's mercurial work in *Jules and Jim,* different from one second to the next and yet a perfect whole. She expanded on it enthusiastically. "Anything carries when you have conviction. You can be totally different or have the moods change or switch from serious to comedy if you believe it, and everybody will go along. One little shred of doubt, though, and you've lost them all, you know? I mean, the strength of the will, the strength of conviction, I don't know, what *is* conviction? Is it red or blue? It's so intangible. What . . . what chemical transmits itself in doubt? One flicker of doubt and everybody—gets doubtful. And most people are followers. They need you to be sure. They might resent you for being sure but they need you to be sure. They would fall apart if you weren't sure."

She isn't altogether as free as she'd like to be yet in her performances; the rehearsals are still sometimes better than the takes. She still worries about the way she looks, and worries about worrying about it. Every actor, man or woman, is a narcissist by trade. The trick is to accept this concern with one's body and put it in the proper place—concern and body both. She thinks of herself primarily as an instinctive actress, and her instincts are indeed phenomenal. Yet she can also get hung up temporarily on irrelevant details—a question of gum chewing or something, or the arcane symbolism of some costume. And this confusion is compounded by the fact that irrelevant details may also be crucial in their way. Barbra has an extraordinary grasp of how costumes can define character, and an actress who's worried about gum-chewing techniques in a particular moment may actually be freeing herself to do the important work in the scene without thinking about it.

Her completed movie work consists of three elaborate musicals: *Funny Girl, Hello, Dolly!* and *On a Clear Day You Can See Forever*, which was directed by Vincente Minnelli. Barbra and musicals have done well by each other. But she's ambivalent about her singing now. She seems to be suggesting that she doesn't want to do any more musicals—no more pat, flat spectacles, the kind with the backgrounds in focus. She knows there are less rigid, less predictable ways of making movies these days, and she'd like to join in the fun. But First Artists, the new movie company she formed six months ago with Paul Newman and Sidney Poitier, has not yet announced a single production, and her own methods for searching out new material are haphazard.

In the meantime, however, she's gainfully and happily employed on *The Owl and the Pussycat*. She plays a hooker, Doris ("I'm an actress and a model . . .") to George Segal's Felix, a pseudo-intellectual, in this version of Bill Manhoff's Broadway play. Neither Barbra, director Herbert Ross nor anyone else connected with it would represent *The Owl and the Pussycat* as a piece of avant-garde filmmaking. It's a romantic comedy, and it's intended to make people laugh. But it does represent a significant step in her career. It's an intentionally small-scale movie being shot under extremely low pressure at several New York City locations and mainly in a dinky studio on Manhattan's West Side. Its characters and dialogue have some basis in reality, if not necessarily in natchelism. It's not a musical, though she hums a bit. She has some near-nude scenes in it and the movie, to her great pride and pleasure, is X-rated.

"Lazy": She even enjoys the unnude scenes. She's at ease with herself on this film. She says she's getting increasingly lazy in her work, but what that means is that she's getting decreasingly compulsive about details that don't matter. Notoriously late in the past, she's a model of promptness on the job. She respects her director and leading man and takes pleasure in a well-founded belief that the feelings are mutual. She likes working in New York, where the men on the crew talk like she does and she can go home after work to her apartment and her 3-year-old son Jason. Up in Central

Park for location shooting one recent afternoon, she looked too pretty to not touch in a brown and white Dynel imitation lynx coat and white boots. She and Segal were shooting a scene in which he throws her to the ground and humiliates her until she cries. The scene was difficult for several reasons. It was freezing cold. A pot of charcoal embers hung under the Panavision camera to keep it warm, but there wasn't any charcoal for the actors. They had to make their wrestling look spontaneous and free while at the same time hitting their marks to be in focus. Finally, Barbra had to cry at the moment that the camera moved in for her close-up.

Even the lowest-pressure production can put the squeeze on an actor. The afternoon sunlight was failing and here they were with nary a wet eye in the house. Cry and the world smiles with you. But she couldn't cry, and she couldn't forget that she was supposed to appear a few hours later at the première of *Hello, Dolly!* at the Rivoli Theater on Broadway. She racked her brain for a way to make herself cry. The device she claims to have found was the thought of how guilty she'd feel if she went to the première of another movie and hadn't done her work properly on this one. It may not be so, but it makes a good story. The fact is that the camera turned, the tears flowed, the shot was made and the girl went home. Smiling.

Willing: "I can't tell you how marvelous she's been," said Ross, a tall, soft-spoken man who has known her since he did the musical staging in *I Can Get It For You Wholesale.* "It all comes out sounding like platitudes, but she's so generous—willing to do it my way or George's way. She has a feeling not that everyone loves her but that she's one of us." He spoke of one scene with Segal and Barbra in bed "where she takes off her bra, and it wasn't easy for her at first. She had so many inhibitions to throw off. You know, 'What would my mother think of this?' Once she did it the first time it was easy for her, but it really cost her."

Ross had directed Peter O'Toole in *Goodbye, Mr. Chips* and he said O'Toole and Barbra were the two best actors he's ever worked with. "She isn't technical the way Peter is, a highly disciplined, highly trained actor. She has this ability to make right choices intuitively. But they're both alike in a way: They're never unprepared. They always know who they are and what they're doing. There may be areas within a scene that she's a little fuzzy about, and sometimes she'll get hung up on a little

97

thing, a trifle, but the essentials are always clear." Before doing this movie, he said, he wouldn't have known what to think about her future. "But now I think her range is incredible. She's really what acting is all about—*being*. The more she tests her range the more expanded that range is going to be."

The most frightening part of stardom, superstardom or whatever the position is that Barbra occupies at this point in her professional life is that it inhibits growth. The historical pattern is plain. A star succeeds, repeats the success, varies the repetition slightly but insignificantly and ends up in a prison of self-parody. The most promising part of Barbra's case is that the pattern may not apply. She seems genuinely eager to test and expand her range, to grow in many directions. If she's only now beginning to be free as an actress, then the best is yet to come.

There would seem to be an undeniable logic to what she's doing now, getting out of those lavish musicals while the getting is good. The studios are collapsing and the studio chiefs, in self-preservationist frenzy, are blaming it all on big-budget productions. The true culprits, however, have been *bad* big-budget productions. *Funny Girl* made a fortune for its producers, despite its initial cost. Thanks to her presence, even *Hello, Dolly!* has a chance of making back its $25 million cost, though the logic of that budget is, of course, indefensible. To judge from the production photos, *On a Clear Day You Can See Forever* has invested a queen's ransom in costumes, as well as salaries, but there's no reason to think the ransom won't be recouped.

Hopefully, Barbra will do plenty of small movies that leave her free to explore character, reality, the finer texture of life. Hopefully, too, though, she'll be able to think big and sing big and work big again if she wants to. It was great fun seeing her on that tugboat with the Statue of Liberty in the background—in focus. It should be greater fun to watch her pump new life into the musical-comedy form and find new ways to use music in movies; any movies. When a girl can sing "Any Place I Hang My Hat Is Home" the way she does, her voice ought to be free to pop out of its cage at will.

1977—Barbra Streisand has been named World Film Favorite for a fourth time in a Reuters News Bureau survey of 60 countries outside of North America. Streisand previously won the award in 1970, 1971 and 1975. Robert Redford lags behind her record with three wins: 1975, 1976 and 1977.

COLUMBIA PICTURES BIOGRAPHY
February 17, 1972

*O*ne of the world's greatest entertainers, at the top of her profession in whatever medium she chooses, Barbra Streisand won the Academy Award as best actress of the year with her motion picture debut performance in "Funny Girl," the William Wyler/Ray Stark production for Columbia Pictures.

Where most stars are content to orbit in carefully established spheres, Barbra Streisand is constantly broadening her range and refining her talent. A leading star of recordings, television, Broadway and Hollywood (with three roadshow screen musicals to her credit in less than two years), she played her first non-singing role with George Segal in "The Owl and the Pussycat," which reunited her with "Funny Girl" producer Ray Stark and Columbia Pictures, and soon will be seen in "What's Up, Doc?," co-starred with Ryan O'Neal.

Look magazine once described Barbra as "the most talked-about, sought-after performer in many, many years" and it is a measure of her perfectionism that the description is even more applicable today. She has been honored more times than any young performer in the world. By resolutely refusing the advice of so-called "professionals" to mold herself in the carbon-copied image of a successful star, she has established herself as a unique personality whose individuality is especially appealing to today's young people.

Although Barbra first claimed attention as a singer at such nightclubs as New York's Bon Soir and Detroit's Caucus Club and through a series of million-dollar-selling albums, she has always described herself as "an actress who sings." Early in her career the New York Times' John S. Wilson noted her interpretive skills: "She has considerable vocal range and such control that she can move quite readily from rough throatiness to a flawlessly pure tone in a single breath. An even more important element, how-

101

ever, is her complete involvement in each song, which enables her to give the song a positive interpretation that in most instances is decidedly original and brilliantly effective."

Her talents as a comedienne first attracted attention when she appeared as Miss Marmelstein, the unnoticed and unloved secretary in the Broadway musical "I Can Get It For You Wholesale." The musical, which opened March 22, 1962—only ten years ago—received mixed notices, but Barbra was singled out for lavish praise: "Brooklyn's Erasmus Hall High School should call a half-day holiday to celebrate the success of its spectacular alumna, 19-year-old Barbra Streisand," wrote the New York World Tele-gram & Sun's drama critic, Norman Nadel, while the New York Times' Howard Taubman called her "the evening's find . . . a natural comedi-enne." For her performance she was named the year's best supporting actress in the New York Critics' poll, nominated for a Tony, signed for a series of recordings by Columbia Records and cast by Ray Stark to play his late mother-in-law, Fanny Brice, in his Broadway production of "Funny Girl."

"Everybody knew that Barbra Streisand would be a star, and so she is," wrote Walter Kerr in his review of "Funny Girl" when it opened March 26, 1964, at the Winter Garden Theatre. All the critics were equally ef-fusive, including Norman Nadel: "A spontaneous comedienne, a big-voiced, belting singer and a brass gong of personality, she set an audience tingling time after time." Her distinctly original musical-comedy perfor-mance won her a second Tony nomination.

Shortly thereafter she signed a ten-year contract with CBS-TV to pro-duce and star in a series of color specials. Her first one-hour, one-woman show for the network, "My Name Is Barbra," proved a resounding success with both the public and the critics. "A pinnacle moment of American show business, in any form, in any period," raved United Press Interna-tional's Rich DuBrow. "She is so great, it is shocking, something like being in love. She touches you to your toes, and then she knocks you out." Originally broadcast on April 28, 1965, "My Name Is Barbra" was re-peated the following October 20th and then was aired in England, Hol-land, Australia, Sweden, Bermuda and the Philippines.

Any doubts that "My Name Is Barbra" (which won five Emmy awards) was a one-shot success were dispelled by her second special, "Color Me

Barbra," on March 30, 1966. As Newsday's Al Salerno wrote, "One Streisand a year won't make a TV season, but it certainly will be awaited eagerly, for its glow will last long beyond anything television provides as regular fare." The *New York Morning Telegraph*'s Leo Mishkin concurred: "It takes a great personality, as well as a first-rate singer, to hold a TV show together for a full hour solely on the sheer strength of her own talents. Barbra Streisand did it magnificently in 'Color Me Barbra.' It's difficult to see how any other television musical show can top it for the rest of this year. Unless, of course, a third Barbra Streisand program is to be scheduled."

Meanwhile, Barbra continued to delight capacity audiences on Broadway, then went to London and repeated her triumph when "Funny Girl" opened at the Prince of Wales Theatre in the spring of 1966. As one critic wrote, "As far as I am concerned, the legend can have erred only on the side of conservatism. Miss Streisand is a miracle." The London drama critics, in Variety's annual poll, voted Barbra's performance in "Funny Girl" the best female lead in a musical for the 1965–66 West End season. Her nine-week London run proved so successful that black market tickets were being sold to the SRO event for as much as $280 a pair.

A veteran of two "command" performances at the White House for the late President Kennedy and for President Johnson, Barbra also dazzled leading Londoners in a special performance at the American Embassy as part of a Festival of American Arts. Almost the entire House of Parliament, along with British government officials and figures from the arts, turned out for an evening that ambassador David Bruce characterized as unprecedented.

Before leaving for London, Barbra had signed a contract for a nationwide concert tour to be made upon her return. Originally scheduled for twenty cities, the tour had to be abridged to four stops when Barbra became pregnant. In each of these four cities—Philadelphia, Atlanta, Chicago and Newport, R.I.—she appeared in huge outdoor stadia in order to accommodate as many Streisand fans as possible, and the audience response was extraordinary. One reviewer wrote of the experience: "Her name is Barbra and there is only one—there really and truly is. She is not a singer; she is The Singer."

After these triumphs, Barbra went into temporary retirement as Mrs.

103

Elliot Gould, mother-to-be. Her marriage three years earlier (September 13, 1963) had culminated a romance that had begun backstage during the run of "Wholesale," in which Elliot was the leading man. Their child, Jason Emanuel, was born December 29, 1966. She and Gould have since been divorced.

Before Barbra began work on her first film, "Funny Girl," she gave a June, 1967, concert in Central Park that drew a record-breaking 135,000 people and became one of the few show-business events to warrant front-page coverage in the *New York Times*. CBS-TV taped the concert and the resulting television show, "Barbra Streisand—Happening in Central Park," was aired September 15, 1968, three days before the world premiere of "Funny Girl."

If there has been a more auspicious performing debut in the history of motion pictures than Barbra's in "Funny Girl," no one can recall it. *Newsweek*'s Joseph Morgenstern, normally one of the most reserved film critics, wrote that "Miss Streisand has matured into a complete performer and delivered the most accomplished, original and entertaining musical-comedy performance that has ever been captured on film." For her screen interpretation of Fanny Brice, Barbra won the Academy Award and the Golden Globe Award as best actress of the year and was named the "Star of the Year" by the National Association of Theatre Owners. These awards joined her many other honors, including several Grammy awards, Cue Magazine's "Entertainer of the Year" award, and designation by the Friars Club as "Entertainer of the Year." She is the second woman to be so selected by the nearly 70-year-old all-male theatrical organization.

Barbra moved immediately from "Funny Girl" to two other films based on Broadway musicals, "Hello, Dolly!" and "On a Clear Day You Can See Forever." She then signed to make "The Owl and the Pussycat," plus a five-year contract with Las Vegas' International Hotel for what Variety called "the highest sum ever paid a performer for cafe appearances."

For actress-singer Barbra Streisand, "record" has always been, and undoubtedly will continue to be, a word with at least two meanings.

"*I* was waiting in front of the Sherry Netherland for Jackie O., when Barbra showed up with her [press] agent Lee Solters and a friend. The friend was an unidentified man, and I didn't attempt to take her picture. The next day, *Time* and *Newsweek* are desperately calling for pictures of Barbra and Pierre Trudeau, [Prime Minister] of Canada. That's who the man was, and I didn't take the picture! I asked Lee, 'Why didn't you tell me?' His answer was, 'Barbra is my client, not you.'"

—paparazzo RON GALELLA

105

STREISAND IS THE DESIGNING WOMAN AS WELL AS STAR OF *THE MAIN EVENT*

"*I*f I hadn't become an actress," says Barbra Streisand, "I would have designed houses, furniture or clothes or been in advertising, or had something to do with the art world."

Now, in *The Main Event*, Streisand has been given the opportunity to delve into this personal love of design as well as to accept the challenge of a new comedic and romantic role.

In one of *The Main Event*'s first sequences, Streisand, who portrays a successful perfume manufacturer, is seen in her plush executive offices. She became personally involved when it was decided that the office would be decorated in an Art Deco motif, with monotone grays and blacks blended in a striking way. Highly familiar with this area of design, Streisand became active in the planning and execution of this setting—to the extent of even having the Art Deco doors from her home transported to the studio for use in this scene in the romantic comedy.

"I can remember my first apartment in New York City," she recalls. "It was a railroad flat on Third Avenue—and I filled it with screens and lacquered chests. Even when I had no money, there was always the need to design my surroundings."

Since those days, Streisand has become an expert on the style of Art Nouveau and Art Deco, as evidenced by the many fine objects and antiques which she has carefully collected and which now adorn her New York penthouse and homes in Los Angeles and Malibu Beach, California. She is quite knowledgeable about the history, origins and similarities between the two creative movements, and continues to study and refine her expertise in these and other artistic modes.

"I really enjoy all periods of design," Streisand notes. "Going back into the past is like little flights of fantasy for me.

"I simply love beautiful things," she adds, appearing as sure-eyed in her sense of design as she is about almost every other aspect of her professional career. "I love precision and perfection—and I like junky things too."

107

Funny Girl, 1968
Hello, Dolly!, 1969
On a Clear Day You Can See Forever, 1970
The Owl and the Pussycat, 1970
Up the Sandbox, 1972
What's Up, Doc?, 1972
The Way We Were, 1973
For Pete's Sake, 1974
Funny Lady, 1975
A Star Is Born, 1976
The Main Event, 1979

All Night Long, 1981
Yentl, 1983
Nuts, 1987
The Prince of Tides, 1991
The Mirror Has Two Faces, 1996

Barbra
the Filmmaker

*B*arbra Streisand.

The name, alone, evokes an image of unsurpassed artistry and amazing versatility.

Never content to rest on her considerable laurels, she is an artist who constantly nourishes, redefines, and underscores her legend by matching her talent with unusual challenges.

"Nuts" is the latest bold and unconventional step in Streisand's phenomenal career, a career etched with a formidable series of "firsts."

For her very first Broadway appearance, in "I Can Get It For You Wholesale," she won the New York Drama Critics Circle Award and received a Tony nomination.

For her very first record album, "The Barbra Streisand Album," she won two Grammy Awards in 1963.

She was honored with an Emmy Award for her first television special in 1965, "My Name Is Barbra."

For her motion picture debut, in "Funny Girl," she won the Academy Award as best actress of 1968.

She was the first female composer ever to win an Academy Award, for her song "Evergreen," the love theme from her hit film, "A Star Is Born."

Undertaking the monumental challenge of making the motion picture "Yentl," Barbra Streisand became the first woman ever to produce, direct, write and star in a major film—not to mention the first person to do so in a musical.

She has also received the most prestigious awards in every medium of the entertainment arts—the Oscar, the Tony, the Emmy, the Grammy, the Golden Globe—as well as countless others, ranging from the French government's Chevalier des Arts et des Lettres (Commander of the Arts and Letters) to being named a fashion innovator on the best dressed list.

Streisand not only stars in her new motion picture "Nuts." She developed, produced and wrote the music for the powerful and emotion-charged drama.

This time she plays Claudia Faith Draper, who was shaped into an angry, anti-social, unconventional woman by a particular set of circumstances. At once worldly-wise and self-destructive, she is brought face-to-face with her own reality and with the society she shuns by committing a tawdry murder. And yet, when the chips are down, she still refuses to play by society's rules.

Streisand was born April 24, in Brooklyn, New York, to Diana and Emanuel Streisand. Her father, who died when Barbra was fifteen months old, was a teacher and a scholar.

An honor student at Erasmus Hall High School in Brooklyn, the teen-age Barbra Streisand plunged, unencouraged, into show business by taking a 50-minute subway ride into Manhattan. Unable to get work as an actress, she entered a singing contest at a small club and won. She soon had a devout and growing following that flocked to the clubs that began hiring her. Before long, she attracted music-industry attention at such spots as the Bon Soir and The Blue Angel.

She signed a contract with Columbia Records in 1962, and her debut album quickly became the nation's top-selling record by a female vocalist.

In 1963, she was signed to play the late, great comedienne Fanny Brice in the lavish Broadway production of "Funny Girl." The moment the curtain came up, the show and star were hits.

"Everybody knew that Streisand would be a star, and so she is," wrote Walter Kerr in his *Herald Tribune* review of "Funny Girl" when it opened at the Winter Garden Theatre March 26, 1964. Her distinctly original musical-comedy performance won her a second Tony nomination.

Her star on an unbridled ascent, she soon signed a 10-year contract with CBS Television to produce and star in a series of TV specials. Her contract gave her complete artistic control—unheard-of at that time for someone that young and inexperienced. The first special, "My Name Is Barbra," earned five Emmy awards, and the following four, including the memorable "Color Me Barbra," earned critical praise and top ratings. These first two specials were recently released, 24 years later, and became best-selling video cassettes.

In the spring of 1966, Streisand traveled to London to repeat her "Funny Girl" triumph at the Prince of Wales Theatre. London drama critics voted her the best female lead in a musical for the 1965–66 West End season.

There have been few motion picture debuts as auspicious as Streisand's in "Funny Girl." Besides the 1968 Academy Award as Best Actress, she won the Golden Globe, and was named "Star of the Year" by the National Association of Theatre Owners.

After "Hello, Dolly!" and "On A Clear Day You Can See Forever," she next chose to star in "The Owl And The Pussycat," released in 1970.

In 1972, after starring in the Warner Bros. comedy "What's Up, Doc?," she made "Up the Sandbox," one of the first American films to deal with the growing women's movement. It was the first picture for her own production company, Barwood Films.

The memorable "The Way We Were" brought her a 1973 Academy Award nomination as Best Actress.

The successful "A Star Is Born," released by Warner Bros. in 1976, was the first motion picture to benefit from her energy and insight as a producer.

In 1968, when Streisand had just completed her first movie, she read a short story by Isaac Bashevis Singer titled "Yentl, The Yeshiva Boy" and hoped to make it her second film. Fifteen years later, the dream came true. "Yentl," a romantic drama with music about a courageous young woman who discovers that in matters of heart and mind nothing is impossible, came to the motion picture screen as a result of Barbra Streisand's legendary persistence and passion. Successful at the box office, it received four Academy Award nominations, and Streisand received a Golden Globe Award as producer of the Best Picture (Musical or Comedy), while first-time director Barbra Streisand was named Best Director of 1984. They represent two of her 11 Golden Globe Awards.

Possessing one of the rarest voices in recording history and a penchant for risking the exploration of different musical directions, the "actress who sings" has continually remained at the top of the charts. Equally at home in pop, show tunes, rock and ballads, she even made a classical album, entitled "Classical Barbra."

Twenty-seven of her albums have become gold, and nine have reached platinum status; she has been honored with eight Grammy Awards.

Her activities in 1986 and 1987 are typical of the energy and talent that have managed to keep Barbra Streisand in the forefront of her profession. In 1986, while she was preparing "Nuts," her compelling "The Broadway Album" was released to near-breathless critical praise and sales in the multi-million bracket. It brought her three Grammy Award nominations, and in February of 1987 she was named Pop Female Vocalist of the Year.

In addition to considerable career demands, Streisand has become a leading spokesperson and fund raiser for her favorite social causes. Over the last 20 years, the only times Streisand has performed in concert have been for causes she believes in. Prior to the 1986 political elections, she decided to help elect several Democratic senators to Congress, and performed her first full-length live concert in 20 years, raising $1.5-million in two hours for the Hollywood Women's Political Committee to disperse to candidates who share her primary beliefs. Taped September 6, 1986, before 500 invited guests at her California home, the concert was titled "Barbra Streisand: One Voice," and aired on HBO December 27, to enormous critical acclaim. With ancillary rights bringing in even more funds, it marked the largest amount of money ever raised by a one-night live performance in California's history.

The "Barbra Streisand: One Voice" profits were channeled through the Streisand Foundation, which occupies increasing amounts of the star's time, energy and resources. The Foundation was set up to support qualified charitable organizations committed to anti-nuclear activities, the preservation of the environment, civil liberties and human rights.

There is a connection between liberties and rights, and the film "Nuts." Streisand says, "In some cases people can be judged insane because two psychiatrists say so. Claudia is difficult, and yes, she makes people uncomfortable. But I wonder how many people have been locked up in disputes over manners? In some countries, people are consigned to mental institutions because they don't follow the social and political line."

Streisand concludes, "People are taking shots at each other on the highways, we're destroying our planet's ozone layer, polluting the water, defacing the globe with a short-term, fast-buck mentality. Now, that's really crazy—that's really nuts!"

A man is commanding—a woman is demanding.

A man is forceful—a woman is pushy.

A man is uncompromising—a woman is a ballbreaker.

A man is a perfectionist—a woman's a pain in the ass.

He's assertive—she's aggressive.

He strategizes—she manipulates.

He shows leadership—she's controlling.

He's committed—she's obsessed.

He's persevering—she's relentless.

He sticks to his guns—she's stubborn.

If a man wants to get it right, he's looked up to and respected.

If a woman wants to get it right, she's difficult and demanding.

If he acts, produces and directs, he's called multi-talented. If she does the
    same thing, she's called vain and egotistical.

—from Barbra Streisand's keynote address

at the Women in Film Crystal Awards, 1992

BARBRA STREISAND AND CHAIM POTOK
Chaim Potok
Esquire, October 1982

On spirituality, fears, illusions, and how actress and writer can best use each other

*O*n a warm autumn night, the stars concealed by high clouds, I am being taken by car to a reception in the home of Barbra Streisand, who sponsored the lecture I delivered earlier in the evening at the University of California in Los Angeles. I carry within me visions of fabled Hollywood parties, feel a deep sense of unease and, at the same time, an openness to this new experience. Also, I have been told that Barbra Streisand is studying Talmud, is supporting a Hebrew school, has celebrated her son's bar mitzvah—activities that are not usually associated with superstars.

I am curious about Barbra Streisand.

Inside the house, all seems a dreamlike landscape as I move through richly furnished carpeted rooms and spacious hallways. Food and drink are in abundance. The decor is luxuriant art deco. The crowd is large but seems no different from party crowds anywhere, is perhaps even more subdued than most. I hear much sober talk about censorship and the Moral Majority. Familiar movie personalities wander about looking startlingly diminished in their prosaic humanness.

Someone takes my arm and steers me into the living room. I catch a glimpse of Barbra Streisand through the crowd around her. The crowd parts and there are introductions.

She is wearing a wide-brimmed hat, a tight-fitting white dress, a shawl. I gaze at the legendary face—the mouth with its slow-curving rises and sudden soft valleys, the startling promontory of a nose, the wide and dreamy pale-blue eyes. Her slight build surprises me, as does her average height; I had thought her to be taller and somewhat more Monroe-like than she is. Until now, if I thought at all about Barbra Streisand, it was only during weary and indolent moments—watching the screen of a jet or, late at night, a television set—when her acting and singing offered me many moments of deep pleasure.

The crowd around us has gone off and we are alone. She tells me that she was at the lecture and liked it very much. We talk. Suddenly she is telling me about her father, who died when she was very young. She is recounting her recent visit to his grave in Queens, New York, and her subsequent discovery of some of his scholarly writings. I listen to her clipped New York inflections, observe her arm gestures, am fascinated by her mouth and faintly antic expressions. She seems a replica in fragile human dimensions of her Olympian screen presence—the charismatic ugly duckling, the Woolworth costume-jewelry clerk amid Tiffany gems. I sense in her the street-smart New Yorker, a native of my own early world, shrewd, sophisticated, vulnerable, demanding.

Somehow the talk has veered to *Yentl*, the movie project in which she is now engaged. She asks if I would like to see some recent location shots for *Yentl* after the party.

When the guests are gone, she brings me into her study, an enormous room furnished with couches, chairs, a large white desk, a white piano, a television set. A few close friends and associates are present. She finds a tape and puts it into the cassette system. The large television screen floods with color.

I see Barbra Streisand as Yentl walking down narrow Eastern European streets in the male garb of a talmudic student. "Yentl the Yeshiva Boy," a short story by Isaac Bashevis Singer, is about a girl who loves to study Talmud. Her mother is dead, and she is raised by her scholarly father, who teaches her behind draped windows and locked doors; girls did not openly study Talmud in the ambiance of Jewish Eastern Europe. After her father's death, Yentl leaves her home town, takes on the guise of a boy, assumes her dead uncle's name, and enters a talmudic academy. Intriguing adventures take place as circumstances force her into playing many roles simultaneously—daughter, man, student, friend, husband, woman—until she finally reveals her identity to the young man, Avigdor, who has become her closest friend and whose former fiancée she has married.

117

Barbra Streisand, approaching forty, looks convincing as Yentl the ye-shiva boy, who is around sixteen in the short story but will be twenty-five or so in the movie.

Later, in the entrance hall, I tell her that I received a call from *Esquire* magazine about a week before, asking me to interview her.

Instantly there is a narrowing of the eyes, a taut guardedness. She pulls the shawl about her, a protective gesture. "I don't give interviews any-more," she says. Anyway, she's too busy now with the movie to give an interview. But she'll think about it.

We are standing at the door. "At least yours would be an honorable interview," she says.

Alone in my hotel room, I find myself intrigued by the encounter. I remember the location shots in which she went about in the guise of a yeshiva boy. A convincing illusion. How do you distinguish between reality and illusion in someone whose professional life is measured by expertise in dissimulation?

It is very late when I am finally able to sleep. As it turns out, it is the first in a number of late, sleepless nights that I will spend with Barbra Streisand.

118

About two months later I am in a 747 over England with my wife, whose skills as a psychiatric social worker will prove useful. We are descend-ing through dense clouds. Wisps of mist break across the wings of the jet. The wet, orderly countryside is barely discernible below.

Early the next day the phone rings and I hear the familiar voice with a New York accent.

"When can I see you?" I ask.

She says, "I don't know. I'm up to my ass working on the script."

I let that hang in a long silence and stare out the window at the dreary London day.

It has taken weeks to arrange this trip, and now that we are here, Barbra Streisand is not certain when she can see me. I wonder what the point is to that? Studied indifference? The antics of superstardom? I hold the phone to my ear and wait.

She breaks the silence. Could I come over tomorrow for a twelve-thirty lunch? She gives me her address. She isn't certain where the house is or what part of London she's living in. She thinks it's called Chelsea. She doesn't go out. On second thought, could I come over at twelve instead of twelve-thirty?

I think to myself that some sort of unspoken message has been conveyed to me in that conversation, and cannot imagine what it might be.

"I'll bring my wife along."

There is a measured pause.

"What'll she do?"

Sunday is cold, and brilliant with sunlight. A cab takes us to a two-story stone house that is painted dazzling white. The heavy brass knocker on the door elicits no response, but almost immediately, a voice on the street behind us calls out, "Chaim!" We turn, and it is Streisand.

She is walking quickly toward us along the street, bareheaded, her gait springy.

"It's such a beautiful day," she calls out happily. "I've been for a walk." She comes lightly up the path to the steps. "I haven't been out of the house all week. I was beginning to feel . . ."

She struggles for the word.

"Entombed," I offer.

"That's right," she laughs. "Entombed."

I notice that she has no makeup on her face save the barest of eyeliner accentuating the pale-blue eyes. The three of us go into the house and climb down a flight of winding stairs to a large den. We settle into the sofas around a low table.

Barbra is wearing a long-sleeved black sweater and matching black knit pants, which are tucked into low black suede mid-heel boots. Around her neck she wears a long, narrow black and ecru-lace scarf. Her reddish-brown hair is caught in a ponytail high on her head, and wisps of hair frame her face. Her long, slender fingers end in unpolished tapered nails. A large, clear, simple stone adorns her left hand; on her right hand is a slender silver ring with a small turquoise-colored stone.

We engage in a few minutes of inconsequential conversation in an atmosphere that feels to me somewhat strained. Barbra tells us that she never talks about herself, never has interviews. I know that she has given some interviews in the past and wonder what she is really saying. "Someday

I want to write a book," she continues, "on account of these crappy books written about me. People think they know all about me. They talk about my love life and they know nothing about me, really." She gives a faint but effectively disdainful emphasis on the word *nothing*. She pauses, then continues. "I can't believe it, but legally there's nothing we can do. I'm public property.

"It's so strange," Barbra continues. "I once read a chapter in one of those books, and they got everything wrong. My favorite composer is Harold Arlen. So they wrote in that book that my favorite composer was Harold Rome. The 'Harold' was right."

Individuals who are intensely engaged in a lengthy period of creativity rarely say or do anything that is not a reflection, consciously or unconsciously, of their focused will and compulsive need to complete their task. "I feel invaded. I feel that people get an impression of me that is not true. I mean, somewhere there is truth about which I'm finding out. When I was very young, they used to say I was difficult. I asked a lot of questions. I was curious in areas that didn't belong to me. Now I'm understanding people a little more." She pauses, then adds pointedly, "Especially this man-woman thing. I mean, the roles we have to play as women. I never understood game playing, because I didn't have a father. I couldn't climb on someone's knee and say, 'Daddy, I love you,' and get a new dress. It's something I've never gotten used to, playing games that way."

It is clear that there is to be no formal interview just yet and that she is unwilling or unable to talk about anything right now that is too far removed from the movie. I understand that feeling; we are an intrusion, and she will talk to us only on her own terms.

"Do you think that Yentl is playing a game?" I ask.

"No," Barbra responds quickly. "I think she refuses to play games. She didn't have a mother and therefore didn't understand those aspects of a woman."

She talks about the movie. At times it is difficult to determine where Barbra ends and Yentl begins; the edges of the two personalities blur, flow into each other. She seems filled and possessed by the work. It is a familiar sensation; novelists know it well.

Abruptly she moves to a scene in which reference is made to two talmudic rabbis, both of whose contradictory points of view were regarded by others as acceptable. She is trying to make sense of this and wishes to use in the scene the notion that life is filled with contradictions, things can be different from one another, opposite, and at the same time good and true.

"Do you know any good things about Hillel and Shammai?" She is asking about two of the earliest and greatest talmudic sages, men of vast learning and differing backgrounds who disagreed with each other about virtually everything.

I tell her that I know a lot of things about Hillel and Shammai.

"Oh, God, could you tell me some?" Her voice is almost childlike with expectation. "I mean if I could just get some of those things." There is a brief pause. She looks at me. "You know, it's like I thought, Why am I doing this interview? Not only because you're a good writer but because you're a rabbi. That's what I thought of this morning. You know what I'm saying?" She regards me keenly. "I want you to help me. I mean, I want to know what you know as a writer and a rabbi." And before I can react, she asks me about a passage in the prayerbook.

I decide to respond. My wife joins in. Soon we are on a labyrinthine voyage through texts, the kind of sacred texts Yentl might be studying secretly with her father. Barbra tells us that she has sought the advice of rabbis. The rabbi of a synagogue in Venice, California, refused her offer of payment for his help and, instead, asked if he could teach her son for his bar mitzvah. "I was very moved by that," Barbra says, "so that's why I support his school."

The talk turns to the subject of the status of women in Judaism. Barbra is analyzing the character of Yentl and relating it to that of the father. She stops suddenly and says, "I don't know if I ever told you the story of how I finally sat down to write *Yentl* after procrastinating for years and years."

She begins to talk about her father.

He was a high school teacher and held doctoral degrees in English literature and psychology. He served as superintendent of schools at Elmira Reformatory, where he taught English to prisoners. He wrote two doctoral dissertations, one a study of Shakespeare, Dante, and others, the second a study of, as Barbra puts it, "my mother's behavior toward her son." She says, describing the second dissertation, "After every chapter there's an analysis of everything that was wrong, the mixed messages my mother was

121

giving my brother. I always had these books, but I could never look through them."

She then proceeds to relate a strange tale.

"My brother is not a dreamer, he's structured right in the world, he's not a spiritualist or anything. My brother was nine years old when my father died; I was fifteen months. So I didn't know my father at all. My brother did. He had told me about this woman friend of his who was a medium, a nice Jewish woman, but who had this spirit that came to her when she was thirteen years old. He said, 'I can't tell you the experience I just had last night. I talked to Daddy.' He said, 'We put our hands on this table and the table moved its legs and started to spell out Daddy's name. Then,' he said, 'the table followed me around the room.'

"Now this is my brother. My brother's not on drugs, my brother lives on Long Island, he's doing very well. So, I believe him. When I came to New York, I wanted to go visit my father's grave. My father died when he was thirty-five years old, but I had never gone to his grave. I was very angry at my father for dying, which is probably why I never read his books. Anyway, I went to see my father's grave, and I had my brother take my picture with the tombstone in back of me. On the tombstone is a Phi Beta Kappa key and the words BELOVED TEACHER AND SCHOLAR. And—you're not going to believe this but next to my father's tombstone was another tombstone. Do you know what the man's name is on that other tombstone? Anshel. Have you ever heard of anyone named Anshel? It's a rare name." (In the movie, Anshel is the name Yentl takes when she assumes the guise of a man.)

Barbra continues talking about her father.

Someone learned of her affiliation with the synagogue in Venice and wrote a letter to the rabbi, saying he had once known Barbra's father. In the letter he described her father in considerable detail.

"My father was a very religious man," Barbra says. "He worked for his parents, who owned a fish store in Brooklyn. He went to New York University and to Columbia Teachers College, and one Friday afternoon he couldn't get home before sundown and he walked back to Brooklyn; he wouldn't ride on the Sabbath. His dream was always to go to California. He wanted to be a writer."

The author of the letter sent Barbra a picture of her father. "I look just like my father," Barbra continues. "I'm built like my father. I said to my mother, 'Why didn't you ever tell me about my father?' She said, 'I didn't want you to get upset. I didn't want you to miss him.' So I never heard about my father. And now I find he was on the debating team, he was interested in drama, he was a member of the chess club. To earn money, he was a lifeguard.

"He was a strange combination—tennis, swimming, Talmud, mathematics club. In fact, I find that I'm like my father and I never knew it. I feel like I put on my father's clothes and became my father."

Her voice is controlled but resonant with what I sense is real emotion. She continues her story, and now the words take a bizarre turn.

"I went back that night after the ceremony and said I wanted that medium to come. She came over and we all sat around and put our hands on this table. The table starts to move a little. I'm very suspicious. I thought it was electrical energy that was moving the table. The legs started to move a little bit. I started to get very scared. I remember I got up and went to the bathroom. When I came back the table spelled out my name. I was so scared. It spelled out S-O-R-R-Y. And it spelled out S-I-N-G. And it spelled out P-R-O-U-D. Then the table stopped moving."

I have always regarded spiritualism as charlatanry. Yet, listening to her, I have the distinct feeling that she is reporting this illusion as a real event that somehow conveyed to her and her brother messages of truth that they both needed to hear. I did not know at the time what to make of her story—and still do not to this day.

During the flight back home, she read her father's dissertations. He began to exist for her, he became real. "I think it has a lot to do with *Yentl*," she says earnestly. "I want to dedicate this film to my father."

OVER lunch that day we talk about the man-woman relations in Jewish orthodoxy. My wife says that much of what passes as religious law in this connection is really not law but a powerful sociological orientation. Barbra picks this up immediately. "That's what I'm saying. It's not law. It's bullshit. Men have used these things to put women in their place."

"Right," says my wife fervently.

"The Church did the same thing," Barbra goes on. "It's that same struggle we're coming back to, this male-female power struggle. I think it

123

also has to do with erections. A man is so capable of feeling impotent that what makes him able to have an erection a lot of the time is the weakness of women, feeling stronger than the woman. What would happen to a society where the women were just as strong as the men? Would there be babies?''

Later that afternoon, she asks if we would like to hear some of the music from *Yentl*. In the den, she puts a cassette into the tape deck of the stereo. Suddenly the air vibrates to the haunting sounds of a dulcimer. The rooms swells with the slightly nasal Streisand voice, its two-octave tessitura richly textured at both ends of the range, now low and soft and breathy, now powerful, now surging. I note how carefully she pronounces her words, the syllables distinct. Her singing and speaking languages are quite different from each other.

The music ends. Then, in response to a question I put to her, she says, "I'm absolutely terrified about being a director. Everybody is talking to me, I have no moment alone. Everybody has to know the answers to everything. I'm getting paid back for all the times I thought I knew the answers. What I'm trying to figure out is how to get joy out of work. If I record, that's a good thing, because it's controllable somehow.

"Movies are design," she adds. "Movies are graphics. I love designing houses; I have seven of them." We have been talking for about six hours and I finally say that I think I will let her rest.

"I'm gonna work now," she announces. Then she says that she would like to see us again. Would I read the new version of the script? She'll have a copy sent over to the hotel.

The message is clear: I give Barbra some days of work on the script, she gives me the interview. Yet, intriguingly, the bait is less the interview itself than it is the world she is trying to portray, my feeling that I ought to help her avoid crude errors, my awareness of the potential quality of the material and its possibility for art. I am disturbed by the I-use-you, you-use-me relationship that she has established between us but, at the same time, am pleased to be able to participate in the film. And I sense that she assumed I would feel that way.

THE NEXT EVENING we are back in the den with Barbra. With us are Alan and Marilyn Bergman, the lyricists who wrote the words for the songs in *Yentl*. The five of us sit in that den for hours, discussing dialogue and scenes, much of the talk centering on the Jewish content of the film—this talmudic idea here, that folkloristic notion there—avoiding any attempt to romanticize the tradition and bearing in mind that the movie must speak to all sorts of people.

It becomes clear to me in the course of the evening that in most matters Jewish, Barbra's knowledge is confused and rudimentary. Yet she asks questions openly, unselfconsciously, with no hint of embarrassment, and takes notes with the assiduous concentration of one long committed to learning. I have no way of gauging the depth of her comprehension. Her mind leaps restlessly, impatiently, from one subject to another; she wishes to know everything, and quickly.

Hours later, my wife and I are in the front hall, putting on our coats. It is close to midnight.

Barbra, standing beside me, murmurs, "I'm not taking advantage of you, am I, Chaim?"

She says this seriously and with no attempt to charm, and I answer that if I felt she were taking advantage of me I would certainly tell her so.

"I am taking advantage of you," she says. And adds, "But we're both really trying to do the same thing."

The next day, seated in chairs and couches around a large, low table that is cluttered with pads, scripts, coffee cups, cassettes, and tape recorders, we begin to talk about the latest script of *Yentl*.

I feel like a character in a bad novel. Everything seems askew, dreamlike, absurdly riddled with the vacuousness of commercial Hollywood illusion and the clichés of forgotten books and movies.

My wife and I have spent the entire day working on the script, augmenting the character of Avigdor and writing a first draft for a new ending. The script was studded with awkward errors—about Jewish rituals, biblical passages, and other such—and we corrected them.

The night wears on.

Hours later, Barbra is reading aloud our version of the ending. It seems to me a flippant reading, words skipped and blurred, passages intoned mechanically as if from a telephone book. She appears unimpressed and unmoved. I am annoyed by her manner of reading. I listen to her and have no notion of what she will do with our suggestions; we will find out when

125

we see the movie. Well, I tell myself, I gave and soon she will give. An equitable arrangement.

SOMETIME LATER, I am alone with Barbra in the den.

"Interview at one o'clock in the morning," she says now and gives a nervous little laugh. We are entering the structured geography of the interview relationship, which she cannot easily control. The air between us, relaxed and informal all through the many script conferences, has become subtly changed.

I begin by asking her this question: "In terms of your art, where do you place yourself? Do you see yourself as a singer, an actress, a fusion of both?"

She tells me that she has always seen herself as an actress and thought that to be a singer was demeaning. The words are followed by a ripple of laughter. "Isn't it awful? It sounds terrible. Even when I was about five or six, I remember singing in the hallways of my apartment in Williamsburg on Pulaski Street, because it made a wonderful sound in the hall. And when I was about nine, neighbors and I used to sit on the stoop together and sing harmonies. I was known as the girl with the good voice. So my mother took me to an audition for MGM. My mother wanted to be a singer, but she was too shy. My mother has a beautiful voice, a very high, light soprano voice. I remember what I wore, too. A blue dress from Abraham and Straus, with white collar and cuffs. I had to sing behind a glass booth. I sang a song, and the guy said thank you, and that was it."

At the age of fourteen she entered acting school. She would go to the Forty-second Street library and look up all the parts that were played by Eleonora Duse and Sarah Bernhardt. In the film library of one museum she saw a movie Duse made in 1916. "She was incredible to me, very real. I never wanted to be a singer."

She began to make the usual rounds as an actress. But that lasted only two days. "People could use their power over me. They had power to treat me like an animal. I had no dignity. I gave up. I just found it so demeaning to say, 'Do you have a job for me?' I couldn't do it. Two days. That was it. I gave up my career. I thought I'd design clothes or something. One day a friend of mine said to me, 'There's a talent contest where you get free meals'—which always interested me. I listened to some songs and I learned one of them, and I entered the talent contest and I won. But when I was singing I always felt, This is not who I am. I'm not a singer, I'm an actress."

Someone from the Bon Soir club was present at the talent contest and asked her to come over to the club and audition in front of an audience. She got her first job.

She remembers taking classes at the Actors' Studio with Lee Strasberg, who never paid attention to her. "I was nobody then," she says. Years later he came to see her in *Funny Girl* and she said to him, "Lee, I don't know what it is. You teach preparation. You know, the actor prepares. I can't prepare. I have to sort of walk on." And he said, "Your preparation is not to prepare. It's okay."

"I never felt part of the world," she says hesitantly. "I mean, I always felt like some sort of outcast. I'm not comfortable with my success. I never was. I don't like to be recognized. I don't know that I'm like a famous person or star. I feel just like a workaholic. Sometimes when I was around people like Sophia Loren or Elizabeth Taylor, they were like stars to me. They're very comfortable with the press, with photographers. You see pictures in the paper of Jackie Onassis or Elizabeth Taylor. They're always smiling like ladies. You see pictures of me, it's like, you know, leave me alone, get outta here, why are you taking my picture? Don't you have any respect? They click flashbulbs in people's faces and you can't see anything. It's not polite. It's not kind. I resent being treated like a thing, a commodity, an image. I don't think I'll ever get used to it."

She wants to be famous and anonymous simultaneously. A wish for irreconcilable opposites: unlimited candy and perfect health; endless blue skies and rain rich valleys; parents forever present and carefree independence. Hillel and Shammai in eternal harmony. I am on familiar terms with that wish.

"You don't see yourself as part of organized society?" I ask again.

"I'm not saying I'm right," she answers. "I'm certainly not particularly comfortable in the world. At this point I live in the cocoon, so I don't even know what the world is."

A pause, a deep breath. The eyes have narrowed, are reflective. She has started to feel very Jewish, she says, and resents the present apparent rise of anti-Semitism. But she is not the kind of person who goes easily to the barricades. "I'm more frightened than most people are. I mean, I want to become more that kind of person, go to the barricades, fight back, and do what I can to change things. But sometimes I think—this is going to sound terrible, very pessimistic—but I do believe that the world is coming to an end. I just feel that technology, science, and the mind have surpassed the soul, the heart. There's no balance in terms of feeling and love for fellow man."

We return to *Yentl*. She can already feel the attacks mounting against her, she says, because she is producing, directing, starring. "Some of the things I've done I'm not proud of. I've done movies at times for the wrong reasons. I want to return to the dreams I never fulfilled. I mean, I really want to do Shakespeare and Chekhov and Ibsen, parts that I've always wanted to play and said I would play but have never gotten around to. I'm tired of saying, 'I could have done this.' I want to *do* it. Because life is growing short. Maybe because my father was so young when he died, I seem to have a drive to get it all in. I want to take chances now. I mean, I want to risk the failure. I want to put my money where my mouth is. I so respect directors and their obligations and responsibilities. It's an incredible challenge."

128

Even more so is the challenge of being a producer. Streisand seems nearly overwhelmed by her financial responsibilities; by her dealings with the unions and with insurance companies; and by the casting process. And she seems obsessive about the problems of production design, makeup, costumes, hair, and every piece of cloth. "Every color is important," she says. "I have to deal with sketch artists, musical numbers. What's awful is that everybody gets to get out of here and I can't leave. My boyfriend goes home, my son goes home."

Yet, in a city rich with theater, she allows herself no diversions.

"I don't like going to the theater," she says. "That sounds awful. That's why I hate being interviewed: 'I don't go anywhere. I don't do anything.' I like to go to the opera and the ballet. I go to the theater and most of the time I don't like what I see. People look at me. I get claustrophobia in theaters. I feel like I have to get out. I have to sit on the aisle." She says that she hated her early experience in the theater. "I liked the rehearsals. I loved changing scenes, changing things, songs, every night, change. But once they freeze it, that's it. You're in prison. That's why I like movies. You do it, it's over; you do it, it's over. You don't have to keep doing the same thing over and over again."

I ask her if she's finding anything in religion at present that she didn't find there before. "Are you returning to it in a serious way?"

She says that she never left it. "I'm a Jewess through and through, although I'm not religious. I don't do anything intentionally to hurt anyone. I feel like I'm a good person. And that feels very Jewish to me. There isn't enough support for Jewish artists and Jewish culture, so I'd like to support that. But I don't go to shul on the Sabbath. I'm not a born-again Jew."

"You feel a loyalty to the Jewish people."

"Yeah. I'm proud that I'm a Jew. I mean, I always like it when I light the Shabbos candles, but I don't do it every Friday night."

Then, as if a signal has sounded a warning inside her that she has been separated too long from her current obsession, she returns to the subject of the movie and the tribulations she has had to endure in order to get the movie made.

I ask, "How'd you finally prevail?"

"I just wouldn't give up. I mean, I had to do it. The more obstacles I had, the more I had to do it. Do you think I'm crazy to, like to ask you to give me a hand, to write, and things like that? Do you think that's terrible to do?"

She did not have to ask me that. I sense genuine feeling in her words and tell her that it is not a terrible thing, that most creative people would like to do all their work alone, by themselves, but sooner or later find that they need the help of others in order to realize their own mysterious and bewildering drives. Sometimes when creative people come together, they establish their relationship—whether they're aware of it or not—on an I-use-you-with-dignity, you-use-me-with-dignity kind of basis.

She takes this in, her face expressionless, her eyes wide and staring, and does not respond.

I say quietly after a moment, "I wish you a lot of luck, Barbra, and a lot of patience."

ALL THROUGH THE journey home and in the days that follow, her face and voice linger in memory and I find that I miss her presence. A certain ineluctable quality of charismatic radiance has brushed against me, and I carry it on a speaking trip to Los Angeles soon after my return. There I talk about her with a number of people.

Those who know her professionally tell me of her prodigious talent, her fits of impatience, her toughness and tenacity, her relentless striving for perfection. Some bemoan her personal life; others say it is no one's concern but her own. A producer tells me of phone calls made by her in an effort to patch up real or imagined hurts. A rabbi tells me of her benevolence to institutions of learning, her honest interest in matters of the mind. A director reaffirms my sense of her basic integrity. In a field not overly sown with seeds of human virtue, she seems something of an unusual and quixotic flower.

As the resonance of the London journey fades, the welcome perspectives of time and distance enable me to attempt some suppositions about her.

She seems to me to be among those creative individuals who find it necessary to construct elaborate stratagems of abnegation that often border on self-torture. This intensifies their misery and thereby, in mysterious fashion, heightens their art.

I sense about her something of the aura of the narcissistic personality: alluring, playing at being charming, centered on one's own self, laboring relentlessly and expecting the same of others, too soon bored with achievement, too quickly disdainful of permanence, grasping at opposites, at times impatient to near ruthlessness with those of smaller mind or lesser vision. This is meliorated somewhat by her self-effacement, her recently reinforced sense of Jewishness, and her awareness that if you pretend to be something you are not, you are nothing.

I think, too, that by fusing her identity with that of Yentl, she is recovering her long-lost father and his religious tradition. She is extending his life and his Jewishness, thereby assuaging a deep sense of guilt at having already lived longer than he. Also, through that extension she is reliving her own childhood as if her father had not died and abandoned her.

It seems clear enough to me that while the movie enables her to continue her father's life and Jewishness through the power of illusion, it gives her at the same time the opportunity to assert forcefully her own creative

130

individuality in the real world. As if in confirmation of this, a cable arrives from her some days after our return from London. The cable reads:

DEAR CHAIM
SOMEONE ELSE'S WORDS BUT MY REASON FOR DOING "YENTL." "IF I DO NOT ROUSE MY SOUL TO HIGHER THINGS, WHO WILL ROUSE IT?" MAIMONIDES. BEST WISHES BARBRA

I. B. SINGER TALKS TO I. B. SINGER ABOUT
THE MOVIE "YENTL"
Isaac Bashevis Singer
The New York Times, January 29, 1984

In the 1950s, Isaac Bashevis Singer wrote a story titled "Yentl the Yeshiva Boy," about a rabbi's daughter with "the soul of a man and the body of a woman." The young woman, Yentl, is so hungry for learning that she defies Talmudic law by disguising herself as a man in order to attend a yeshiva, or religious school. The story, set in 19th century Poland, was adapted for the stage in 1974 and recently became the basis of a big-budget Hollywood musical produced and directed by Barbra Streisand, who also plays the title role. Herewith, Mr. Singer asks himself a few questions about Ms. Streisand's "Yentl."

Q: Have you finally seen the Yentl movie?

A: Yes, I have seen it.

Q: Did you like it?

A: I am sorry to say I did not. I did not find artistic merit neither in the adaptation, nor in the directing. I did not think that Miss Streisand was at her best in the part of Yentl. I must say that Miss Tovah Feldshuh, who played Yentl on Broadway, was much better. She understood her part perfectly; she was charming and showed instinctive knowledge of how to portray the scholarly Yentl I described in my story. Miss Streisand lacked guidance. She got much, perhaps too much advice and information from various rabbis, but rabbis cannot replace a director. The Talmudic quotations and allusions did not help.

Q: Did you enjoy the singing?

A: Music and singing are not my fields. I did not find anything in her singing which reminded me of the songs in the studyhouses and Hasidic *shtibls*, which were a part of my youth and environment. As a matter of fact, I never imagined Yentl singing songs. The passion for learning and the passion for singing are not much related in my mind. There is almost no singing in my works. One thing is sure: there was too much singing in this movie, much too much. It came from all sides. As far as I can see the singing did nothing to bring out Yentl's individuality and to enlighten her conduct. The very opposite, I had a feeling that her songs drowned the action. My story, "Yentl the Yeshiva Boy," was in no way material for a musical, certainly not the kind Miss Streisand has given us. Let me say: one cannot cover up with songs the shortcomings of the direction and acting.

Q: Is it true that you wrote a script of the play which Miss Streisand rejected?

A: It is true, and when I read her script and saw the movie I understood that she could not have accepted my version. In my script Yentl does not stay on stage from beginning to end. The leading actress must make room for others to have their say and exhibit their talents. No matter how good you are, you don't take everything for yourself. I don't mean to say that my script was perfect, or even good. But at least I understood that in this case the leading actress cannot monopolize the stage. We all know that actors fight for bigger parts, but a director worth his name will not allow one actor to usurp the entire play. When an actor is also the producer and the director and the writer he would have to be exceedingly wise to curb his appetites. I must say that Miss Streisand was exceedingly kind to herself. The result is that Miss Streisand is always present, while poor Yentl is absent.

Q: How do you feel about the writing?

A: It is not easy to make a film from a story. In most cases, it is impossible. The great plays such as Shakespeare's, Moliere's, Ibsen's, Strindberg's were written as plays. My Aunt Yentl used to say to my Uncle Joseph, "In a pinch I can make from a chicken soup a borscht, but to make from a borscht a chicken soup, this is beyond any cook." Those who adapt novels or stories for the stage or for the screen must be masters of their profession and also have the decency to do the adaptation in the spirit of the writer. You cannot do the adaptation against the essence of the story or the novel, against the character of the protagonist.

Let's imagine a scriptwriter who decides that Mme. Bovary should end up taking a cruise along the Riviera or that Anna Karenina should marry an American millionaire instead of committing suicide, and Dostoyevski's Raskolnikov should become a Wall Street broker instead of going to Siberia. This is what Miss Streisand did by making Yentl, whose greatest passion was the Torah, go on a ship to America, singing at the top of her lungs. Why would she decide to go to America? Weren't there enough yeshivas in Poland or in Lithuania where she could continue to study? Was going to America Miss Streisand's idea of a happy ending for Yentl? What would Yentl have done in America? Worked in a sweatshop 12 hours a day where there is no time for learning? Would she try to marry a salesman in New York, move to the Bronx or to Brooklyn and rent an apartment with an ice box and a dumbwaiter? This kitsch ending summarizes all the faults of the adaptation. It was done without any kinship to Yentl's character, her ideals, her sacrifice, her great passion for spiritual achievement. As it is, the whole splashy production has nothing but a commercial value.

135

"To Barbra Streisand: The Queen of Tides . . . You are many things, Barbra, but you're also a great teacher . . . one of the greatest to come into my life. I honor the great teachers and they live in my work and they dance invisibly in the margins of my prose. You've made me a better writer, you rescued my sweet book, and you've honored me by taking it with such great seriousness and love.

"Great thanks, and I'll never forget that you gave 'The Prince of Tides' back to me as a gift. Pat Conroy."

—inscription from the author in Barbra Streisand's copy of
The Prince of Tides

136

BARBRA! SCRATCH THE NAILS
Paddy Calistro
Los Angeles Times, January 17, 1992

*D*irector Barbra Streisand allowed actor Barbra Streisand to be a bit heavy-handed in *The Prince of Tides*. That's not a complaint about her acting—it's about those fingernails. Those very long nails with the very French-tipped manicure.

For every person talking about Nick Nolte's superb performance or the film's sensitive story line, there's someone else talking about the nail gaffe. At a time when short, tailored nails painted red or buffed to a natural shine are the trend, Streisand's old-fashioned talons stuck out.

"Her nails upstaged her entire performance," said screenwriter Ellen Shepard. "It's hard to believe no one suggested that she take the focus off her hands." A press agent, who asked not to be identified, called the hand scenes "narcissism, pure narcissism." And at least one viewer walked out of a recent screening after Streisand, portraying a serious psychiatrist, let out a ditzy "Oh, no, my nails!" when Nolte threw a football to her.

The director-actress-singer has worn her fingernails very long since the late '60s, when polished claws were fashionable. On her "The Way We Were" album cover, circa 1974, her nails appear straight on and in silhouette. And in every Streisand film except *Yentl*, in which her character tries to look like a young boy, her trademark nails are never far from view.

So what? Psychologists—amateur and professional—are having a field day with interpretation.

"She wants us to understand her power and control," said Beverly Hills manicurist Rando Celli, who tends the nails of Faye Dunaway, Diana Ross and Rickie Lee Jones. "Those long, strong nails say, 'Keep your distance.'"

"She has beautiful hands and wants them to be noticed—and look, everyone's talking about them," said skin-care specialist Ole Henrikson.

"Women who aren't comfortable with their appearance often fixate on one feature that they like and take special care to call attention to it," said Glendale psychotherapist Christine Maginn.

Brentwood psychologist Fanya Carter agreed: "Streisand's hands are her one special feature; if she calls attention to them, she distracts audiences from her nose. But this time . . . too much attention to her best feature made her insecurities show."

"*H*er most striking characteristic is her personality, more than anything physical. I love her profile. I love her attitude. I hate her attitude. She reminds me a lot of having an older sister, where you want to love her and then at times she can be such a perfectionist it just annoys you no end. You have this ongoing battle Streisand has with the press: She absolutely can't live without publicity, but she hates it."

—photographer FRANK TETI

1995—When Barbra Streisand watched the NBC television premiere of her film, *The Prince of Tides*, she became convinced that the commercials were louder than the program. She telephoned the station engineer from her home and demanded he equalize the volume.

"Take it down 2 db's," she instructed. "I'll take full responsibility."

He did. And she did.

THE STREISAND-MIDLER CONNECTION
Marlene Adler Marks
The Jewish Journal, January 2, 1992

Why our two most successful Jewish actresses drive us crazy

The release of two "Christmas" films, *The Prince of Tides* and *For the Boys,* provides us, ironically, with a glimpse of the changing status of America's two greatest Jewish female stars, Barbra Streisand and Bette Midler.

Do you blanch at that description? Streisand and Midler are far more than "Jewish female stars"; they are universally acclaimed icons, who, to use the cliché, "belong to everyone." Streisand's and Midler's popularity is no more a product of their Jewishness than Magic Johnson's adoration as a basketball player stems from his being black.

And yet, it seems to me that today's film audiences—and especially American film critics—bring to performances by both of these women expectations and assumptions that have very much to do with a precise Jewish past, however unspoken or unconscious those expectations may be. That past, rooted first in the conventions of Yiddish theatre, vaudeville and then on Broadway, continues to dictate to us in the audience long after these theatres themselves have stopped being pertinent to our lives.

These poor ladies are damned if they do, damned if they don't. Midler gets panned for being too vaudeville, too schmaltzy and "over the top," while Streisand gets criticized for running from musical comedy, as if she were still Miss Marmelstein (of *I Can Get It For You Wholesale*) and could do nothing else.

In *The Prince of Tides,* Streisand stars, directs and produces the abridged film version of Pat Conroy's bestselling novel about the love affair between Tom Wingo, a wounded Southern man (Nick Nolte), and his suicidal sister's New York psychiatrist Susan Lowenstein (Streisand).

Rather than concentrating on Streisand's obvious gifts as a director of a film with minor epic grace, or her achievement in guiding the magnetic performance of Nolte, what drives critics (among them syndicated commentator Tom Shales of *The Washington Post*) absolutely nuts is her refusal to sing.

ROOTS ARE IN VAUDEVILLE

Where does such stereotyping begin? Oddly enough, though vaudeville itself has been dead 50 years, vaudeville-style comedy is only now taking its last breath. The historian Irving Howe suggests that vaudeville-style comedy is a predominantly Jewish humor designed to "shake off the immigrant experience." Earliest "shakers" were, of course, Al Jolson, George Jessel, Milton Berle, the Marx Brothers, Fanny Brice, Sophie Tucker and so on. Their comedy, says Howe, was based on three major ingredients: ethnic embarrassment, extravagant gestures and the desperate need on the part of a large number of Jews to succeed in show business at all costs. This was broad, sight-gag humor (often done in blackface), which evoked in its largely immigrant audiences passionate attachment to the stage personality of the actor: George Burns's cigar, Jack Benny's cheapness, Jolson's Mammy.

But after vaudeville died, an interesting thing happened: Ethnic-based Jewish humor, marked by the same hyperactivity and frenzy to succeed, found popular acceptance in movies by, among others, Mel Brooks (*Blazing Saddles*) and Paul Mazursky (*Down and Out in Beverly Hills*). The conventions of vaudeville remained, especially the humor to be found in contrasting the (Jewish) city slicker with the country bumpkin. This is the hub of Neil Simon's best comedies, *The Odd Couple* and *The Sunshine Boys*, as well as such cult films as Carl Reiner's *Where's Poppa?*

But while the male vaudeville comic gave way in later generations to the American film director/writer, women did not make that easy transition. This is the Streisand-Midler problem. Audiences still relate to these women through the easily recognizable ethnically identified singer/comics they loved early on: Miss Marmelstein/Fanny Brice for Streisand,

142

the Divine Miss M for Midler. Any change in form is considered treason.

Since her Broadway days ended, Streisand has been constantly knocked for her determination to make such films as *Yentl* and *The Prince of Tides*. Her public interviews read as exercises in self-justification and self-definition, explaining herself as a "perfectionist" or an obsessed person, rather than merely a film director with a story to tell. Did Paul Mazursky have to explain his own transition to film directing from acting?

(To be fair, the hype surrounding every Streisand project is so large and full of hubris that the director is never evaluated on a normal scale. *Yentl* is an overblown effort, operating at the level of high-pitched hysteria that Irving Howe would recognize. Such is not the case with *The Prince of Tides*, in which Streisand the actress sometimes seems either asleep or dead inside, while everyone around her is achingly alive.)

If Midler, 45, and Streisand, 49, have always seemed to belong to a much older generation, it's probably because the form of their work—the stage and non-rock music—is of a bygone time. They are not Madonna, with a new hair color a month. And so they are perceived as dinosaurs: not Sophie Tucker's granddaughter, but Tucker herself, surprisingly still breathing.

143

STAR VEHICLES

What then of the new films themselves? I loved them both, with appropriate caveats that these are star vehicles, character studies rather than full-blown stories.

It was during Midler's *For the Boys,* a film that carries us over 50 years of American history, that I began to think about Sophie Tucker, the famed "Last of the Red Hot Mommas." Playing Dixie Leonard at 70 with her upswept blonde hairdo and her sly "I've been everywhere baby" wink, Midler makes explicit her own direct link to Tucker, who long after her days with Ziegfeld (she starred in the follies of 1909) and her career as a singer of black jazz double-entendre lyrics were over, was personifying the slightly randy Jewish grandmother. Tucker, like Midler, made a career out of the outrageous and she must have taught the Divine Miss M a thing or two, especially about how to keep an audience: Right up to her death in 1966 she was making periodic appearances to sing her anthem, "Some of These Days."

Dixie Leonard starts out young, fresh and talented, loving show business, her country, hoping for the future. One after the other, everything and everyone disappoints her. As Midler ages into her osteoporosis and increasing layers of makeup, she heaves and sighs, has nightmares and a tantrum or two. And then she goes out and sings. Her Dixie Leonard becomes the personification of American female adaptability, ultimately dissatisfied with her choices but finally blaming no one but herself for making them. There is wisdom in this performance, perhaps a woman's kind of wisdom, which is why every woman I know has loved this picture. Critics be damned.

CULTURAL DIFFERENCES

For *The Prince of Tides*, Pat Conroy wrote the screenplay based on his novel so we can't say exactly who has gutted the book, which was one-fifth the love story and four-fifths about Tom Wingo's sordid family life. Here the proportions are reversed, but I didn't really mind since it was the love story that interested me from the beginning. (There is some background that is confusingly absent from the movie, but not enough to ruin it for a non-reader who sat beside me.)

Streisand says that this film is about a man who finds the "child within," to quote her guru, John Bradshaw, and learns to forgive his parents. Nonsense. This is a film about cultural differences in America: about New York as being a foreign country to a Southern boy, and how finding (temporary) love with a Jewish woman can make a man feel more at home with his own true self. (We can only wonder who wrote the lines Lowenstein mumbles to Wingo when he's about to leave her: "I'm going to have to find myself a Jewish man. You guys are killing me.")

Streisand makes a fine archetypal New Yorker, though not a convincing psychiatrist, and Nick Nolte is in splendid shape, oozing sexuality and Southern-boy charm. The photography by Stephen Goldblatt (who also did *For the Boys*) is lavish and both South Carolina and New York look great. I'm ready to accept Midler as Sophie Tucker and Streisand as a storyteller. What's the choice? We're gonna miss these red hot mommas, some of these days.

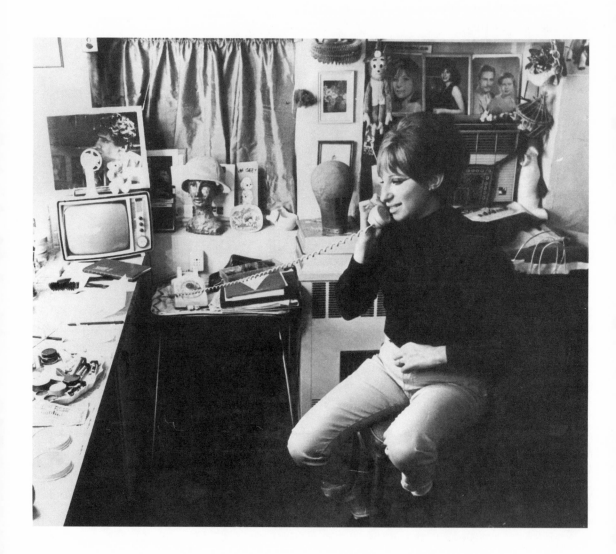

Barbra
the Person

COLOR BARBRA VERY BRIGHT
Rex Reed
The New York Times, March 27, 1966

While Streisand sings, the world stops. She is only 23, yet her name is spoken around the home as often as Jello. The money she makes would put a dent in the national debt. Her first TV special was a milestone. Her second should have even greater impact. She turns records into gold, theaters and concert halls into mob scenes and on TV alone, during the next 10 years, she will make $5-million plus. To hear her sing is like getting the message from special delivery.

Her success, like most successes, brings pressures with it. For one thing, she hates being interviewed, distrusts all photographers and is as nervous about publicity as she is about her own performances. Reporters covering her second CBS-TV special, "Color Me Barbra," to be shown this Wednesday night, 9–10 P.M., even had running bets on just how late she would be for each interview. The answer was almost always: very.

The damp, gray hotel room in Philadelphia is charged with tension. The reporter's date was for one o'clock; it is nearly three. Somewhere, in a suite high above, Barbra is pasting sequins on her eyes. She wanted Pablo of Elizabeth Arden, but he takes too long. Barbra hates to sit still that long. In the corner, a kindly CBS press agent pours Scotch from a bottle sent up by room service. People come and go, telephones ring mysteriously. Everyone smiles nervously. The taping is scheduled to begin at the Philadelphia Museum of Art in two hours. "Barbra is very unpredictable; to tape songs for the show, we rented a studio from 7 to 10 last night; I got home at four A.M.," says the press agent wearily.

MORE SUBTLE

People drop by to give opinions. "She sings more subtly now," says her personal publicity girl, a pretty blonde with pierced ears. "She used to sing her guts out; at the end of 'Happy Days' she sounded like she was screaming. She'd never do that now. When she was in 'Wholesale' she used to beg the press agent to get her interviews so she could get a free meal. Reporters used to stare in horror at the table piling up with hors d'oeuvres, three appetizers, two soups, celery tonic, tomato juice, a main course, and four selections from the dessert tray. Now everything's going so smoothly she only worries about details, refinements. She knew her work so well in 'Funny Girl' she never worried about the singing, but about the dust on the plastic flowers or why the blue light failed on Cue 82. Her closing night she was still giving notes to the orchestra on what they were doing wrong."

Word comes, from on high, that the star is ready for her audience. Three-and-a-half hours late, she plods into the room, falls into a chair with her legs spread out, tears open a basket of fruit, bites into a green banana and says to the reporters, "Okay, you've got 20 minutes."

What's the new show like? "Like the old one. They're like book ends. The first one was great, ya know? So this one's gonna be close as it can be. What do I know from TV? I hire the best people in the business, then I let them do everything for me. I don't take chances. I'm paying the bill, it's my problem, right? I coulda got some big name stars to clown around just like everybody else does on their specials, but who needs it? I got complete creative control here, so I do it my way, right?"

How will the show differ from last year? "Instead of Bergdorf's, the first part's in a museum," she says, munching on a bunch of grapes. "I move around in front of the paintings and sometimes I turn into the paintings, get it? The costumes are mostly designed by me, borrowed, rented, or re-made from my old hock-shop wardrobes. The second part's in a circus, and I sing to all the animals. The last part's the concert. Just like last year's. Different songs, same feeling."

Eight people have moved into the room. All of them check their watches and make her very nervous. Some of them answer her questions for her. "Barbra does not like the image that comes with being a glamorous star," volunteers one. "She doesn't like parties; she's afraid people ask her because she's a celebrity, not because they like her."

"Yeah, like this party for Princess Margaret, you know? Elliot, my husband, even wore a tuxedo. We were so miserable we cut out for a Ninth Avenue delicatessen, my favorite restaurant, where they still got great greasy french fries and the best rice pudding in town. No raisins, you know what I mean?

"Listen, all my life I wanted to be famous. I knew from nothing about music. I never had a Victrola 'til I was 18. I used to buy clothes in thrift shops. Now I don't go there anymore because people bother me. Besides, they've gone up. I always dreamed of a penthouse, right? So now I'm a big star I got one and it's not much fun. I used to dream about terraces, now I gotta spend $500 just to convert mine from summer to winter. Let me tell you, it's just as dirty with soot up there on the 22nd floor as it is down there on the bottom."

At 5 P.M. the museum closes and the cameras are ready. An armada of armed guards line the doors with name tags for everyone official. Disgruntled reporters and unhappy photographers line up in a Renaissance hallway for clearance. "Barbra gets very upset if anyone who isn't official watches her," says a cameraman. Outside, the Philly branch of her fan club peers through the beaded glass windows carrying a sign that reads, "Welcome Barb." "Barbra even has a fan club in prison," offers the press agent.

OP-ART GOWN

At 7:30, Barbra emerges in a floor-length, op-art gown of hand-sewn sequins in 20 colors and six-inch triangle earrings with bolts of lightning through them like Captain Marvel emblems. Mondrian eyes sharpened with mascara and boyish hairdo slicked back behind her ears, she is ready for the first number. A 25-man production crew, a trained nurse, her personal staff and a few favored members of the press watch as bongo drums blare from portable speakers and Barbra shimmies past walls filled with Cézanne watercolors and Matisse still-lifes shaking on their brackets. The number is repeated a dozen times before choreographer Joe Layton bounces through in white tennis shoes and white turtle-neck sweater crying, "It's awful. It needs work."

By 9:30 the test pattern is adjusted and the color cameras are ready for the fourth tape of the first song. A cameraman crushes out a forbidden cigarette on a valuable piece of 100-year-old Rumanian oak while a guard isn't looking. "Let's go, Barb!" "I gotta get up?" cries the star. Hard looks from Joe Layton. Barbra gets up.

"She's not dumb," says a CBS official. "She heads two corporations—one packages her specials, pays her everything, then the profit she makes is the difference between her expenses and what CBS pays her. This includes her salary. It's a one-woman show, so it would be very weird if she was not the boss."

By 11:15 she comes out in a floor-length black satin maid's outfit with white over-apron, which she designed herself. Elliot Gould, her husband, arrives, wearing an official label so the guards will let him in. Barbra runs past 12 pillars and up 35 stone stairs singing "Yesterdays." Then she collapses in a corner eating hot pastrami, sour green tomatoes, kosher pickles and stuffed gefilte fish from paper containers. "My gums hurt," she cries. The crew throws color cables over the balcony of the museum's Great Hall, missing by inches a valuable Alexander Calder mobile and a priceless 17th-century Flemish tapestry. A museum official screams.

Barbra's manager, Marty Erlichman, comes over. Marty is a friendly, bear-like fellow who discovered her at the Bon Soir fresh out of Erasmus High School, a smart, skinny, big-nosed girl who had a 93 average and a medal in Spanish. When he met Barbra he was a little-known talent agent working on Broadway. Now he heads his own company. "For nine months I tried to get her a job. Every record company in the business turned her down. 'Change the clothes, change the nose, stop singing the cockamamy songs.' Now it'll start all over when she hits Hollywood to make *Funny Girl*. They'll want to make her into Doris Day. But she sells the public Barbra, nothing else. She's never been bastardized or exploited. The main thing she's gotta learn is not to trust too much. The public is very fickle. Ten million people love you when you're an underdog on the way up, but nine and a half million of them hate you when you hit the top."

FANS APPEAR

At 2 A.M. a group of teenagers appeared at the museum with a kettle of hot chicken soup. "Just give it to her," they yell through the locked doors. "Could she just wave?" Barbra is busily chewing sour green apple gum (her current favorite) in a lavender and silver Marie Antoinette costume with lavender wig and purple ostrich plumes. "Get rid of them. They follow me everywhere. Sometimes they get my autograph three or four times in one night. Whatta ya think they do with all those autographs?"

The action continues through the next day, with no sleep. Barbra works very hard. Others stop to rest, but her extraordinary energy carries her through. Barbra playing a guillotine scene in the French Revolution. Barbra doing "something based on Nefertiti." Electricians and reporters curl up on tabletops and behind potted palms, catnapping. "If the star gives up, everybody gives up. I gotta keep smiling," says Barbra.

Gradually, the bits and pieces, the long shots and closeups, the takes and retakes that make up a smooth-looking show, are assembled.

Back in New York, part two was achieved through sheer tenacity. Barbra danced out onto a three-ring circus set. A baby elephant named Champagne roared so loudly that a baby llama nearby did a somersault. Barbra sang "Funny Face" in an orange ringmaster's costume. The horse reared. The penguins got sick under the hotlights and had to be carted off to a refrigerated area behind the set. The leopard refused to pose.

Barbra had to worry not about being trampled to death but when to come in on cue. The show was behind schedule and the overtime was costing the star money. Four electricians chased a pig across the set and damaged part of the backdrop. The only light moment came when Barbra sang to an anteater named Izzy. "He must be Jewish," she said, as they touched noses.

More than 30 hours were spent on the circus segment, which runs only a few minutes on screen. Barbra's temper exploded. "Too many people not connected with the show." "Too many people staring at me." The press was removed to the control room.

By week's end there was nothing left to tape but the concert portion of the show. Barbra came out in a pale creamy gown with pearl drop earrings and pale lipstick, standing on a white spiral staircase under blue-turning-lavender lights, switching on the charm for an audience of teased hair girls and screaming teen-age fans—clowning, joking, kibitzing with her little dog Sadie ("a hooked rug that barks"). The magic shone through. Barbra became the public figure—gamine, appealing.

By midnight some 200 hours of hard work were over. The grips packed up, the set was struck. "Great show! She'll make millions on the re-runs," said a control-room engineer. "Give me Julie Andrews any day," said an electrician, wiping his forehead. In her dressing room, the star of the show was told she could finally go home to bed and, for the first time that week, Barbra Streisand was on time.

BARBRA STREISAND: "SADIE, SADIE, MARRIED LADY . . ."
Rona Jaffe
Cosmopolitan, April 1969

This may be the first article to capture Barbra as she is

I first met Barbra Streisand at a party, before she had opened in *I Can Get It For You Wholesale,* or had appeared at the Bon Soir, cut a record, or been married. Very few people had ever heard of her. Our host said to me: "Go talk to Barbra Streisand over there; she doesn't know anybody." She was standing in the corner—a skinny teen-ager with a Modigliani face, wispy hair, and a funny peasant dress. She was with Elliot Gould and they were holding hands, watching the festivities they were no part of, like two scared kids. She was so shy that making conversation with her was like getting blood out of a matzo, but I could see from her face that she was grateful someone had made the effort.

A few minutes later, a girl who identified herself as a press agent of Barbra's came up to me, giggling, and said: "Barbra Streisand thinks she's flat-chested so she's got the front of her dress stuffed with tissue paper—you can hear it crackling. Go look." I didn't. I thought, what a mess it was to be just starting out in show biz and have to put up with people who said things like that to make one sound interesting.

When Barbra first appeared in a night club—the Bon Soir in Greenwich Village—I went down to see her. She was sharing the bill with a female impersonator named Mr. Lynne Carter, and the place was only half-full. I got a table at ringside and sat through two shows, mesmerized by that marvelous voice, the impassioned face, the expressive hands with the long fingers and Dragon Lady nails. I had no doubt then that Barbra Streisand was going to be a big star.

October 1968: I drove up to Barbra Streisand's rented house, in Beverly Hills, which she has leased for three or four months to make her third film, *On a Clear Day You Can See Forever.* It was a superstar mansion, the kind you see in the movies, hidden from the road by a long driveway and spacious grounds. I was relieved to see that none of the cars in the driveway looked very imposing; there wasn't a Bentley or a Rolls in sight. The rent on the house must have been high: the landlord let Barbra build a tall, ornate, white wooden fence around the swimming pool so the baby wouldn't fall in. There were rooms upon rooms, housing Barbra, husband Elliot Gould, their twenty-two-month-old son, Jason, a baby nurse, a full-time secretary, a dresser, a Chinese chef—and Sadie, a fat, fluffy white poodle. I was with Barbra's publicist, David Horowitz, a nice *haymish* man—the kind of unusual press agent you *ask* to stay for the interview.

The house was exquisitely furnished by its owner, film director George Axelrod, with antiques, some kooky things, and original paintings by famous modern artists, and there were lots of windows overlooking the gardens. While I was waiting for Barbra to come downstairs, I went into the huge kitchen, where her Chinese chef, Felix, was making homemade eggrolls, the hors d'oeuvres for an entire homemade Chinese dinner. He gave me one to sample, and it was as different from "takeout" as Maxim's is from Horn and Hardart. Being one myself, I knew then that the Jewish kid from Brooklyn had indeed found success and happiness: homemade Chinese food whenever she wanted it instead of waiting until Sunday night to go to Flatbush Avenue.

As I sat in the living room, drinking beer and waiting for Barbra Streisand, I thought about all the things I already knew about her. People who didn't know her but had read her interviews said she had changed. They said she was an imperious, rude monster. People who knew her well said she hadn't changed. She was still shy. Hardworking. Professional. Adamant about things that mattered. *Right* about them. It took her a long time to make a new friend. She had to trust the person first. She was wary of the new people who flocked around her now just because she was a star, when nobody had wanted to bother with her before. Her best friends were still her oldest friends: Sis Korman, occupation housewife, who comes to visit her often and stays long; her manager, Marty Erlichman (Barbra had once said: "Other people love money, but Marty loves me"). I remembered I had met Barbra one time backstage during the intermission of *Funny Girl*, on Broadway, and she had talked to me about literature, because I suppose that's what most people think they should talk to authors about, and she had said she liked Dostoevsky and Chekhov. And she said that she never had time to read a whole book anymore and it made her feel guilty to have all those books piled up in her bedroom at home and be unable to finish them. And, I thought, how many people would just have said: "I read your book and loved it," when they hadn't read it at all.

Now, in Beverly Hills, she came into the living room and we shook hands, which is a dumb thing for two girls to do but is the kind of thing you feel like doing when you met Barbra. "I'm glad you're late," she said, "because I'm late."

Her hair was long and straight, parted in the middle, blondish brown, and she was wearing the new look in makeup: very little, subtly applied. Her face is softer than it appears in photographs, and quite gentle. She was wearing a navy-blue long-sleeved shirt, matching wide-legged slacks, a beige sleeveless Bonnie Parker sweater, some antique chains around her neck, and bone-colored high-buttoned shoes.

Barbra went to the bar to get a Tab because she's on a diet. "Last night I was dying for some crappy won-ton soup," she said. "Not *good* won-ton soup, and not *really* crappy won-ton soup, but medium crappy, the kind we used to get in Brooklyn, where the kreplach are chewy, not mushy. I can't find it in Los Angeles."

157

She sat down and lit a cigarette. "I have to lose eight pounds and I just can't. I'm O.K. in the morning: I have my skim-milk milkshake with the diet coffee syrup, eighty calories, and then I do exercises and swim in the pool, and then I'm so crazy I just go and eat a whole container of Wil Wright's coffee ice-cream—two hundred calories for half a scoop!"

I complimented Barbra on her shoes and she said, "I got them in Paris. They're last year's, see the pointy toes? They wanted me to go to Paris to pick out the clothes for *On a Clear Day,* but I just couldn't shlep over there and take the baby. So I'm going to have the costumes made; Scaasi for the modern ones and Cecil Beaton for the old ones. I think it's crazy the way they spend so much on clothes for movies when you can just buy them in boutiques." She jumped up to write something down on a piece of paper and sat down again.

"Those shoes look as if they ought to have roller skates attached to them," I said. "Where did you learn to skate so well for *Funny Girl?*"

"In the Brooklyn gutters," Barbra grinned. "But that's the extent of it, I can't skate any better than that. I used to go to the Roller Dome, you know, inside, where you rented skates, and my dream was always to have a pair of my own . . ." The grin turned wistful and she shrugged. "But I never got them. I wanted the good kind, with shoes, not the kind you clamp on that tear the sole right off your shoe like *that*."

I remembered my own Brooklyn childhood, where you always wore a skate key on a string around your neck as a mark of status and roller-skated to the penny candy store on the corner instead of walking, even though it was half a block away. For years I had scabs on my knees, also a mark of status in those days.

"On top of everything, Howard Koch [her *On a Clear Day* producer] just sent me seventeen different flavors of ice-cream from Baskin-Robbins," Barbra said. "Did you ever have licorice ice-cream? Peanut-butter-and-jelly ice-cream? Later, you can taste it. I sent him a note." She looked at her watch. "The baby should be up soon and you can see him. He's so smart—twenty-two months old and he knows all the letters, and he knows all the words to my songs, and he can chew gum! Did you ever hear of a kid twenty-two months old knowing how to chew gum and not swallowing it?

"He saw me chewing it and he said 'gum,' so I took it out of my mouth, and after he chewed it a while I told him to give it back, and he did. Now he chews it all the time. It looks so strange. I let him come on the set once when we were filming *Hello, Dolly!*—the scene with a lot of kids dancing with umbrellas, where they're doing 'Put On Your Sunday Clothes.' Now, whenever he hears any music, he wants to dance, and he says 'umbrella.' He thinks you need an umbrella when you dance because he saw that number. I don't like to take him to the set, though. He came one other time, when we were doing the 'Hello, Dolly!' number; there was me, his *mother*, in a red wig and a gold dress, with a strange man on each side of her, and he got upset. He didn't like it. I got embarrassed with him watching me. It was like having my mother watch me—I can't let her see me perform, either—because she *knows* I'm just pretending and it's not really me at all. Ooh, what is that—*dust?*"

She jumped up and began to dust a leather chair with her hand, then she went to the French doors and began to run her finger over the frame, looking for more dust. "Well, don't you want to ask me any questions?"

"No," I said. "I just sit around with the person."

"Don't you take notes?"

"No. I just remember it all."

"Yeah? Well, I have a pretty good memory, too, and I remember most everything I say, and some of these interviews I read that are supposed to be about me—I never said those things. I don't know why, you come out here and all of a sudden they *hate* you. Those reporters have a journalistic concept, and they just write what they wanted to write before they met me. They write about me as if I'm some kind of an old-fashioned *star*, with an *entourage*. I don't have an entourage. I hate having people around me. I hate people fussing over me."

She picked at a broken nail. "I have a terrible memory when it comes to personal things, but I always remember everything that concerns my work. I can remember something someone said about one of my songs *four* years ago. But at home I have to keep lists all over the house, and every morning I go around gathering up all the lists and then I still forget something, because I forget where I put the lists. You noticed when I jumped up just before to write something down?" She showed me the piece of paper. It said: CLUB SODA.

"The thing about my interviews," she went on, with a rather wry, resigned melancholy, "is that none of them are really me. They're not what I'm really like. I have this friend, Ernest Lehman, who produced and wrote the screenplay for *Dolly!* and a lot of other things, and who's a very nice man, and he said to me: 'Barbra, if they knew what you're really like, they wouldn't write about you.' Because I'm *nice*. But if they knew that, they wouldn't write about me."

The phone rang. It was Elliot, calling from the set where he'd just started work on a new picture. "It's called *Ted, Alice, Carol and Bob*," Barbra said. "That's not the right order, but I always put Ted first because Elliot's playing Ted."

"I heard you were doing a new record album," I said.

"Well, I'm supposed to be, but I've only recorded three songs. I'm lazy."

"Are you a Taurus?"

"Yeah! How did you know?"

"Lazy and musical. Strong, a lot of drive."

159

"Elliot's a Virgo. What's Virgo?"

"Selfless and analytical. Critical."

"Somebody did my chart once but I don't remember it. Do you want to see the baby? Then you can taste the ice cream."

We went upstairs to the nursery, a series of rooms down the hall from the master-bedroom suite. The baby was running around. He has huge eyes and blond ringlets, and it's hard to tell at his age which of his parents he most resembles; he looks like both of them. He ran over to his phonograph to put on a record of one of Barbra's songs. The song, from the as-yet-unreleased soundtrack of *Hello, Dolly!*, went something like: "I'm a woman who always gets my way . . .'"

"Oh, do you want to hear that again?" Barbra said, obviously wishing he'd play something else.

"That," he said firmly.

Barbra started to play a picture-puzzle game with twenty-two-month-old Jason, a game where you had to fit a cutout of an animal into a space and then find and put the name of the animal under the picture. He got every one right.

Barbra then asked Jason to find all the letters and put them into a box as she called them off, and he did that one unerringly, too. "I hate to sort of show him off," she whispered, "but you can't help it, you're so proud of them. When I was pregnant I found some beautiful antique letters made of ivory, in New York, and I bought them for him, so that's how he learned, because he played with them." (I noticed that most of the time we'd been together she spoke without accent, reserving that comedic Brooklyn dialect that is her trademark for her few moments of humor and for public appearances. Does a car salesman sell cars at home?)

Taking the baby along, Barbra showed me around the rest of the upstairs. She has a room to make up in—there was a phonograph there, and the baby put a record on right away. He seems to thrive on music, and when it's playing he can't stand still. Although Barbra had dressed and made up just before she met me, I noticed that everything was put away on the dressing table, in antique boxes and holders.

"You're neat," I observed.

She looked embarrassed. "Yeah."

On the couch in the huge bedroom were some dresses with the tags still on that she'd bought at Ohrbach's. "Isn't that cute?" Barbra said, holding one up. "Like a school uniform. I'm going to wear it with knee socks and flat shoes. They each cost $17.99. It's crazy, I'll buy a Galanos dress, $750, wool, and then I'll go out and buy all these dresses for $17.99. Let me show you my favorite room."

We went into a room that had nothing in it but Barbra's clothes; one wall just for dresses, one wall for shoes, one for bags and accessories. Everything was immaculate. Many Beverly Hills mansions have the same arrangement, but it's still the one thing, to my mind, that speaks of having arrived. For a girl, it's a dream room.

"Mommy's clothes," said Jason.

"Yes," Barbra said happily. "Mommy's clothes." She seemed much prouder of his sentence than of the clothes or the room. She picked Jason up and stood in the doorway.

"Your hair is the same color as the baby's," Horowitz observed. "Does she or doesn't she?"

"You know she does," Barbra said.

She put the baby back in his room and we went downstairs, where Barbra circled the living room, seeing that everything was ready for her dinner guests, wondering where all the ashtrays had got to. She had a *sotto voce* consultation with her housekeeper. I eavesdropped, of course.

"I have these two bra slips that split when they were washed," said the star who makes a million dollars a picture, "and I thought we could cut off the slips so I could still wear the bras so they wouldn't go to waste."

She took me into the kitchen. Strange, exotic Chinese food was laid out on the butcher's-block table, ready to be prepared. "I used to work in a Chinese restaurant," Barbra said. "In Takeout." She rattled off some Chinese. "That's 'sweet and sour pork.'" More Chinese. "That's 'egg roll.'"

She gave me a dish for the ice cream, but we both ended up eating it out of the paper containers with two spoons—licorice ice cream, peanut-butter-and-jelly ice cream, pumpkin ice cream. Then she ran over to the cabinet. "Taste this." She put into my mouth: pickled scallion. "Try this— pickled radishes from Japan. Now we've had everything: pickles and ice cream."

A gift service had sent a sample: a mix of blue cheese and Roquefort

161

rolled in a ball and covered with chopped nuts. Barbra had to open it and try it right away, so we had some of that, too.

"Wasn't that nice of them to send it!" she said.

"They want an autograph," the housekeeper said.

"Everybody wants something," Barbra said, and shrugged.

I left then, with heartburn, and a very warm feeling for Barbra. "Goodbye," she said at the door. "Take care." But the way she said it, it didn't sound like a cliché; she really meant it. Our visit—and it really was a visit, not an interview—was all relaxed and simple. Barbra Streisand really is a nice lady. If she weren't so talented and such a star and didn't say such kooky things, nobody would bother to write about her. But they would be awfully glad they had met her and spent time with her. I was.

Sadie, Sadie, married lady, you can come to my house and eat *hazerei* any time!

BARBRA STREISAND'S INSTANT COFFEE ICE CREAM

INGREDIENTS
[24] marshmallows
[1 cup] milk
[1 tsp] instant coffee
[1 cup] heavy cream, chilled

DIRECTIONS

Turn your refrigerator to the coldest point. Pour the milk into a saucepan, heat, and gradually add the marshmallows. Mix until the mixture is smooth, and then add the instant coffee. Let it cool a bit.

Whip the cream until stiff; mix cream and marshmallows; mix together and pour into an empty ice cube tray. Freeze.

MAKES {4} SERVINGS

THE PRIVATE WORLD OF BARBRA STREISAND
Nora Ephron
Good Housekeeping, April 1969

The funny little girl from Brooklyn has made it oh-so-big in movies, TV and onstage. But she'd rather talk any day about two-year-old Jason and Sadie, the poodle, than dwell on her fantastic success

*T*he house she is renting in Beverly Hills, California, is one of those funny Spanish houses, covered with tile and gingerbread, nestled in hills full of bougainvillea, and chock full of the things she loves: a freezer jammed with coffee ice cream, a glass case of her *art nouveau* objects, a picture of her son sitting naked in the swimming pool, a box of chocolate-covered pretzels.

Upstairs, Jason, who is two years old and chews gum, was taking a nap. His mother was downstairs in the living room, curled up on the couch while the sun dappled off the backyard pool. She was talking about the problems she was facing in raising her child.

This is Barbra Streisand, superkook, I kept telling myself. This is the girl who used to drift about in antique shoes and feather boas . . . who used to drive her Bentley up to Ninth Avenue in New York to buy hot pastrami sandwiches that dripped grease all over the leather upholstery . . . who identified herself in her first theater-program biography as having been born in Madagascar, raised in Rangoon and educated at Erasmus Hall High School in Brooklyn. Any minute now, I told myself, she will get up, drape some ostrich feathers around her neck, and begin to swing from the hall chandelier. Barbra Streisand is a kook, isn't she?

As a matter of fact, she's not. Or if she is, there was no sign of it on the recent afternoon I spent with her. For one thing, she wasn't wearing anything the least bit bizarre: she appeared in cocoa pants, a beige silk overblouse, and a beige-and-brown scarf demurely knotted around her neck. What's more, she didn't look anything like an amiable anteater, or a seasick ferret, or a furious hamster—as she has been described—but rather more like a painting by Modigliani—elongated, elegant. And we actually sat around and talked about such zany things as motherhood. And Dresden china. And dieting. And the price of cooperative apartments in New York. And the teenage years when Barbra was so skinny and shapeless she used to stuff socks into her brassiere and toilet paper around her hips.

"What's she like?" my husband asked me when I got home after seeing her, expecting, I'm sure, something kooky.

"You won't believe this," I said, "But she's this perfectly normal girl who happens to be a movie star."

"I don't believe it," said my husband.

But it's true. Barbra Streisand, who is twenty-six years old and a recording star, stage star, television star and movie star, would much rather talk about the almond duck she is having for dinner than the film she has just completed (Ernest Lehman's *Hello, Dolly!*) or the film she is about to begin shooting (*On a Clear Day You Can See Forever*). Barbra Streisand, who has a cook, a nanny for Jason, a personal maid and a private secretary, gets carsick in the backs of limousines (for no apparent reason), and refused to hire a chauffeur while she was appearing on Broadway because it cost her twelve dollars a week less to take taxicabs. Barbra Streisand is truly delighted at the critical response to her performance as Fanny Brice in the film *Funny Girl* but she appears unable to imagine that anyone would contemplate giving an Academy Award to a kid who comes from Brooklyn.

"Did you see that prophet on the Mike Douglas Show?" her press agent asked her during our interview.

"No," said Barbra.

"He predicted you'd win the Oscar."

"I can't take that seriously," she said.

"He's never been wrong," the agent persisted.

"I'll be his first mistake."

In fact, when you get right down to it, Barbra Streisand, who is, along with Julie Andrews, one of the biggest stars to emerge in the last ten years, would like most of all to spend the afternoon talking about Jason.

Jason Emanuel Gould, that is, who was born at the tail end of 1966 to Miss Streisand and her husband, actor Elliot Gould. Jason is a long,

166

skinny, talkative child who sounds exactly like his mother and looks exactly like his father. Barbra can talk about Jason for hours on end.

She will tell you that she checked into New York's Mount Sinai Hospital to give birth under the pseudonym of Angelina Scarangella; that Jason cried before the umbilical cord was cut; that he eats raw mushrooms, swallows his chewing gum, and puts the tape recorder speaker into his mouth. Naturally, she thinks he is a genius.

"I was just talking to Rosalind Russell for fifteen minutes," said the press agent. "For two minutes we talked about business. Guess what the other thirteen minutes were about?"

"Jason," said Barbra, laughing. And without bothering to explain why her friend, Roz Russell, was as preoccupied with her son as she was, Barbra was off again on the subject of what Jason has to say about grapefruit ("Ooooooo, sour") and how Jason always says okay with a question mark after it ("Okay?"). She beamed. She glowed. She turned serious. "You really see at this age that every mistake you make has an imprint on your child," she said. "It's a terrible responsibility, but a very exciting one."

Thoughtfully, she explained in what ways she was raising Jason that were different from her own upbringing.

"I would *never* lie to him," she said. "And if I make a commitment to him, I have to follow through. My mother would be about to take me to the movies and something else would come up and we wouldn't go. That's terribly unfair to a child, and if you do it often, he'll never believe you. I never force Jason to eat, and he really enjoys his food. My mother always forced me—I was a pathetically skinny kid and I used to go to health camps and have tonics. Those camps were the most horrible experiences of my life. I'd get there, they'd dump me in the bathtub, and then put me into uniform. I hated it. From that time on, I always got allergies in the summer anytime I went to the country. They were psychological in origin, of course.

"Another thing about Jason," she continued, "is that I will always encourage him to do what he wants to do. My mother never encouraged me." She paused. "And yet, if she had, I never would have ended up doing what I am doing. I suppose it turned out better for the world than for me. Subconsciously, I'm always trying to please my mother, which it happens

167

I can never do. It's very difficult. I suppose you have to rely on the inborn nature of the child. I don't know what I would have been like if I had had a normal childhood with a living father. Maybe I would have had the same drives. Jason has a mother who works. Who's to say whether that's bad or good? At least he'll have some respect for me as a human being. At least he'll realize his mother is a person. Then it won't be so devastating when he finds a flaw. It won't be so terrible when he finds out that his parents are just as fallible as anyone else."

How Barbra acquired an image as a kook is not really too difficult to understand. Seven years ago, when the blue-gray-eyed girl burst out of Brooklyn, with a bump on her nose and a spectacular voice in her throat, the press fell in love with her.

She was graphic. "Success," she said once, "is having ten honeydew melons and eating only the top half of each one."

She was uncommonly frank. "When I sing," she said, "people shut up. What can I tell you?" She was occasionally hilariously inarticulate. "Creativity is a part of perversion, like a thing that goes inward for emotion, not responsibly, because intellect is bad for what I do. Know what I mean?" She patronized thrift shops and rhapsodized over stuffed baked potatoes. "But," says Barbra, "I was never that kooky. It was all very logical. When I first sang, I wore a brocade vest I'd bought in a thrift shop, and people looked at me like I was a nut. Was it really kooky? I never did it for effect. I only did it because I got the most for my money in thrift shops. But when people started saying, 'You gotta go see this girl who sings in nutty clothes,' I immediately changed. I never wore those clothes again. I was a singer and I wanted them to watch me sing."

But about two years ago, when she went to Hollywood to make her first film, *Funny Girl*, the gossip columnists declared war on Barbra Streisand—mostly on the theory that what was up must be brought down. The kooky image was replaced by one that was a great deal more harmful in its inaccuracy: it painted her as a snobbish, stingy, monstrous movie star. "Don't believe anything you read about me," Barbra said once. By the time I got to California to see her, I had come to believe she was right.

I had spoken at length with her friends and colleagues, and according to them, Barbra was shy, not snobbish; lavishly generous, not stingy; an obsessive perfectionist, not a monster. Yes, they admitted she was often late. Yes, they admitted she did have difficulty palling around with the crew and making little jokes with them. "She's never read Dale Carnegie," said one of her associates, referring to Carnegie's book, *How To Win Friends and Influence People.* But none of these failings explained why the press seemed so determined to lynch her.

"I don't know what it is about her that antagonizes people, but I suspect it's jealousy," said actress Kay Medford, who worked with her in *Funny Girl.* "When I read some of the stories about her, I feel like a mother tiger."

Had success spoiled Barbra Streisand? Or changed Barbra Streisand? Or done anything at all to Barbra Streisand? No, said her friends. And her personal manager, Marty Erlichman, told a story to prove the point.

"A while ago," he said, "I made a deal for Barbra. She has a dog named Sadie, and I got an offer from a dog-food company to do a picture book on Sadie, along with a record of two dog songs by Barbra. It would have taken her two hours to do and they were going to pay her $120,000 for it. I called her up and told her. 'Barbra,' I said, 'next Tuesday if you come into Columbia Studios from two to four in the afternoon, you can pick up $120,000.' 'I can't do it,' she said. 'I'm going to the movies that day.' She hung up. A half hour later, she called back very upset. She had just bought a lot of presents and she had found out from a jeweler that she could have gotten each of them for four dollars less somewhere else. All in all the difference came to sixty-four dollars. I couldn't believe it. 'You're talking about saving sixty-four dollars,' I said, 'and I just told you where you can make $120,000!'

" 'Marty,' she said to me. 'I *understand* sixty-four dollars.' "

And what about Barbra Streisand's feud with Walter Matthau? Didn't that prove she was a monster? Not according to what I heard. People who worked on *Hello, Dolly!* insisted that Matthau was to blame for the difficulty. "It's a very simple story," said a friend of mine who was there. "She's twenty-six years old and she's the biggest star in town. Can you imagine how a big spoiled baby like Matthau reacts to playing second fiddle to that?"

I didn't even have to imagine it. I knew. Matthau reportedly became so upset he went to complain to Richard Zanuck, the head of 20th Century–Fox. "Do I need a heart attack?" asked Matthau. "Do I need an

169

ulcer?" Zanuck listened politely, until Matthau finished whining. "I'd like to help you out," he replied, "but the film is not called *Hello, Walter.*"

Nevertheless, the press has persisted in casting Streisand as the heavy and Matthau as the poor put-upon creature. All of which has made Barbra Streisand understandably reticent about giving interviews, and thoroughly paranoid about the press.

"If I were to fight back at the misquotes, and the out-and-out lies that people said about me, I'd never get any work done," she said. "I don't want to be thought of as some kind of crazy, mad star who reverts to the Twenties in terms of temperament. Do you know that one writer said on television that I threw candy wrappers over my shoulder while he was interviewing me? Even in my worst days in Brooklyn, I never threw candy wrappers over my shoulder."

The days in Brooklyn are well behind Barbra Streisand today. She is still penny-wise and pound-foolish, but her clothes are from Arnold Scaasi, not the thrift shops that line Manhattan's Second Avenue. In the old days, she used to carry all her belongings around town in a satchel and sleep wherever there was an extra bed; today, in addition to the rented house in Beverly Hills (which belongs to comedy writer George Axelrod), she has a New York apartment on Central Park West—a large apartment, mind you, but not quite large enough for a family of three, the domestic staff and crates of Barbra's cranberry glass. "We wanted to break into the apartment next door," said Barbra, "but the manager of the building wouldn't let us break through a wall. It would have ended up that my son was living in a different apartment from us! Can you imagine him growing up and trying to explain *that* to his analyst?"

When she returns to New York after completing *On a Clear Day,* Barbra plans to plunge into finding a new apartment. She had looked in the fall, found one she loved in an exclusive New York cooperative, and was turned down by the owner-residents of the building who rule on applicants.

"It's an unbelievable experience to be discriminated against," she said. "I guess it was a combination of our being Jewish and being in show business. I was once asked if I'd ever been discriminated against, and I said, 'No, I've never applied to a country club.' But that was before this happened. You know, the board didn't even give me an interview. They apparently think theatrical people are noisy. Let me tell you, it's the society people who are swinging from the chandeliers. We happen to live very quiet, conservative lives. We hardly ever entertain. It's ironic. Now that I have the money to buy an apartment, I might have to live in Los Angeles because they won't have me in New York."

Barbra's life *is* quiet and conservative—dull, in fact, by the show-business standards. When she is working, she spends most of her day on the set, comes home to son and (until recently) husband (who has just completed one film, and can currently be seen in another, *The Night They Raided Minsky's*). After dinner, she spends much of the night on the telephone talking to colleagues about the next day on the set.

The Gould marriage has had its shaky moments—what with long separations due to career conflicts. In February, the couple was reported to be seeking a legal separation. Most of their friends are willing to speculate on the cause of the difficulty. Said one friend: "Obviously there's the problem of her being more successful than he is. In addition, Barbra is so obsessed with her work that she sometimes forgets about the other things in her life."

Even during less stormy times, the Goulds were seldom seen at night-clubs or discotheques, preferring to spend their evenings at home. She loves to poke around antique shops; she takes lessons in French; and she exercises once a day as part of a somewhat futile weight-watching regimen. "It's impossible for me to diet," she said. "Absolutely impossible. If it weren't for my exercise teacher, I don't know what I'd look like. There's nothing that can make me stop eating. I'm fine at breakfast. I'm fine at lunch. But then I get this terrific urge and the most important thing in my life becomes coffee ice cream with cream topping." She laughed. "The cream topping is dietetic.

"I have to lose ten pounds. After all, here I am in the movies." She grinned and repeated herself as if she couldn't quite believe it. "I'm in the movies. What kind of vanity is this? I'm in the movies. If I weren't, it wouldn't matter. But here I am. I had three double chins in *Dolly*. I kept telling people it was because Dolly should be statuesque, but it was a cop-out because I couldn't diet. Of course, you can't see my double chins in the movie. It's a trick I learned from Elizabeth Taylor's cameraman. He told me if you hold the cameras up high and shoot down, you don't see the double chins."

Diets. Double chins. Apartment hunting. And as the afternoon wore on, there was talk of Sadie, the poodle. And natural childbirth. And the broken-down Bentley. And how to order two egg rolls in Cantonese. And the lady who makes the best spaghetti sauce in the borough of Brooklyn. As I said, she's this perfectly normal girl who happens to be a movie star. You'll have to find your kooks somewhere else.

"I'm sure if she had her way, she'd want to see every shot in exchange for standing there. And then she'd say, 'OK, you can have these two back, the other three I'm keeping.' If she could arrange that, she would. Then everybody would get their pictures. But she can't control the elements away from her sets. On a set, she sees everything. Outside, in public, she can't do that. So she thinks, if I can't control it, you're not going to get any."

—photographer SANTIAGO RODRIGUEZ

STREISAND'S RELIGIOUS REVIVAL
Michael Medved
Los Angeles Herald-Examiner, April 1980

*M*y *shul* will never win an architectural award.

It occupies a crumbling, turn-of-the-century building on the ocean-front in Venice; originally, the structure housed a bakery and a shoe repair shop. Over the years, elderly congregants arranged the interior of the synagogue according to their memories of Eastern Europe. The simple *bima* is surrounded by four pillars of painted wood. Primitive murals depicting lions, harps and scenes of Israel decorate the walls.

It is far from elegant, but an unmistakable sense of cheerfulness pervades the place.

One Saturday afternoon in January, a young man of 13 came to the Torah for the first time. Nervously, he recited the traditional Hebrew blessing. Behind him, a red-haired woman leaned forward, concentrating her full attention on the boy.

The young man stood beside his father and grandfather while the rabbi read from the Torah scroll. Touching the appropriate spot on the parchment with the fringe of the *tallis* (prayer shawl) his father had given him that day, he pronounced the second blessing. As he uttered the last syllable, cries of "*Mazel tov!*" arose from the congregation, and a shower of hard candy descended on the boy. Friends and family began clapping and singing enthusiastically. The young man, beaming, ran down to the woman's side of the synagogue, found the woman in the first row, and kissed her warmly.

Barbra Streisand hugged her son. Elliot Gould stood on the *bima* and smiled.

The Hollywood community has never been celebrated for the fervor of its Jewish commitment. That Jason Gould should have experienced a bar mitzvah at all is surprising. That his parents should have chosen an obscure Orthodox synagogue in Venice—with no pomp, no organ, and no professional cantor—is stranger still. . . .

From adolescence onward, Streisand enjoyed only the most casual contact with organized Judaism, yet somehow an unfocused hunger for spiritual fulfillment continued to haunt her. At one point she made a cursory exploration of Eastern religions, and even studied yoga. She also recorded a best-selling Christmas album. All the while, she made no attempt to escape identification as a Jew, in public or in private.

Her interest in Jewish history, in fact, led her to buy screen adaptation rights to an Isaac Bashevis Singer short story some 12 years ago. This occurred long before a Nobel Prize helped Singer gain the widespread recognition and popularity he enjoys today. She bought the property against the nearly unanimous advice of business associates and Hollywood experts. Conventional wisdom dictated that no one would pay to see a feature film that told such a bizarre story of religious Jews in long-ago Poland.

It was "Yentl" that first introduced me to Streisand. She had heard through the industry grapevine that I was not only what passes in Hollywood for a "hot young writer," but that I am also an observant Jew. A meeting was arranged by our respective agents.

We met half a dozen times. Streisand seemed particularly intrigued by descriptions of my congregation in Venice: More than 80 families have moved into our beachfront neighborhood, to rebuild the synagogue, open a full-time day school and launch an ambitious program of adult education. I told Barbra about the leadership of a remarkable 32-year-old rabbi named Daniel Lapin.

Through a strange coincidence, Barbra's mother, Dianna Kind, happened to hear about Rabbi Lapin at the same time I was meeting with her daughter. Mrs. Kind—a vibrant, strong-willed woman in her early 70's—had recently celebrated her own bat mitzvah. This experience raised her concern, in the manner of Jewish grandmothers everywhere, about the Jewish education of her grandson. She suggested Rabbi Lapin's name to Barbra as a possible bar mitzvah tutor for Jason.

Lapin—tall, athletic, fair-haired and blue-eyed—is light years away from the conventional stereotype of an Orthodox rabbi. Born in South Africa, educated in Great Britain and Israel, he is a licensed pilot, an accomplished skin-diver and an ardent sailor who has taught physics on the college level.

After an hour of conversation—about Judaism, the theory of relativity, reincarnation, marine biology and Beethoven's fourth piano concerto—Streisand and Gould felt comfortable enough with Rabbi Lapin to air their concerns about Jason's bar mitzvah. Must the boy memorize long, dreary passages of Hebrew? Would the ceremony have to be a gala event? How many months would Jason have to spend in preparation?

Rabbi Lapin reassured them. Jewish law, he explained, requires only three steps for a bar mitzvah: that a young man be called to the Torah, that he recite two brief blessings, and that he undergo some kind of meaningful education concerning the substance of Judaism.

Jason—a sensitive boy with a beautiful, thoughtful face and surprisingly world-weary manner—still remained doubtful about the whole project.

Two weeks later, I received a call from Streisand's personal assistant, telling me that Barbra would be visiting our congregation on Friday night. . . .

After Jason Gould started his weekly bar mitzvah lessons with Rabbi Lapin, Streisand felt the entire procedure would be empty and hypocritical unless she pursued her own Jewish education along with her son.

So the rabbi arranged for Barbra to study with him for several hours each week. "She turned out to be one of the brightest and most sincere students I've ever taught," the rabbi said. "She has a natural, almost innate facility for Jewish learning."

When word got out that Barbra Streisand spent several hours each week studying with an Orthodox rabbi, Hollywood cynics suggested that she was only looking for free background briefing for her upcoming film. Lapin points out that most of the subjects covered in their discussion bore no possible connection to "Yentl."

As the day of the bar mitzvah approached, Streisand began to show concern that Jason's private ceremony might turn into a public circus—with curious spectators, members of the press and uninvited guests flocking to our *shul*. With that in mind, the specific date, time and place of the ceremony remained a closely guarded secret. Fewer than 50 people attended services, nearly all of them members of the Streisand or Gould families.

The party at Barbra's Malibu ranch, after the conclusion of the Sabbath, offered a dramatic contrast to the modest proceedings at *shul*. More than 200 guests—including James Caan, Neil Diamond and Ray Stark—rode special minibuses from a parking lot near the coast to Streisand's hideaway in the hills. There, three art deco tents provided room for drinking, eating and disco dancing.

Streisand took the trouble to provide a full table of strictly kosher food, as an alternative to the gourmet Chinese buffet offered to most of the guests. To make sure that the rabbi and Mrs. Lapin, my wife Nancy and myself would feel comfortable, Barbra even bought a new set of glass dishes for the occasion.

Before the end of the party, Streisand circulated through the crowd to greet each guest personally. When she arrived at our table, she thanked Rabbi Lapin warmly. And then she turned to me.

"That Jason is really something else," she said. "Know what he told me? He said, 'This party tonight, this is Hollywood. But in *shul* today, that was for real. It was really OK.'"

In the days following the celebration, Barbra made it clear that she is also for real. She is, for one thing, continuing her studies with Rabbi Lapin. At the same time, she maintains her interest and involvement with the Venice community.

Our new Jewish day school, which opened its doors last September, has especially benefited from her support. In view of Streisand's backing—amounting to nearly 20 percent of the school's budget this year and including a long-term commitment through 1984—the institution will be renamed in honor of her late father, Emanuel Streisand.

And so . . . what should we make of all this?

It would be easy to dismiss this as an example of mutual manipulation—of Hollywood stars and Orthodox activists using one another for purely selfish reasons.

I have already heard some snickers from resentful quarters in the larger community concerning Streisand's connection with our congregation. This argument maintains that she chose the Venice *shul* because she wanted to see her son bar-mitzvahed as quickly and painlessly as possible. According to this logic, the shabby little *shul* on the ocean might be considered quaint or chic, and might even serve as a bizarre conversation piece for La Streisand and her elegant friends.

This worst-case scenario fails to explain Streisand's personal commitment to a program of Jewish learning; no one ever demanded that she pursue her own studies in Torah. The cynics will also have a tough time explaining her determination to make a film of Isaac Bashevis Singer's "Yentl." As it happens, her association with Venice comes at a time when she is taking an unprecedented professional risk to produce a movie of genuine Jewish content. Nor does Streisand's heavy and continuing involvement in our day school square with the notion that her recent Jewish explorations are only a passing fancy.

The facts of the situation permit only one conclusion: Barbra Streisand's recently rekindled interest in traditional Judaism is absolutely sincere. Anyone who discusses the subject with her for five minutes will see her passion and her hunger.

I am reminded of a haunting story she told me about her childhood. As a little girl, she had a friend whose parents were self-proclaimed atheists. At age 6, she and this friend used to engage in lengthy discussions about the existence of God, with Barbra's companion insisting that the whole notion was ridiculous.

One afternoon they sat together on a Brooklyn fire escape, watching the street traffic below. Barbra, on the verge of tears, tried desperately to convince her friend of the existence of a deity.

"I know he's there, I know it," she pleaded, and pointed to a gentleman in an overcoat on the pavement below. "I'll prove to you that God is real. He'll prove it to you. Because right now—just at this moment— that man down there is going to turn at the corner and cross the street."

To the absolute astonishment of Barbra and her friend, the gentleman in question did precisely that.

"I've never forgotten that afternoon," says Streisand. "And the last couple of years, it keeps coming back to me. I've always had that kind of special relationship with whatever it is that's out there."

That special relationship continues. And Barbra herself has decided to cross the street.

J had never been a busboy before. But then, I'd never been to Barbra Streisand's home either. My invitation to the songbird's soiree didn't come on a classy cassette, enclosed in a potpourri-filled tin like her guests', but as a message on my answering machine. "You interested in working a party Saturday, September 6, at Barbra Streisand's?" There are, after all, certain advantages to a four-year career as a waiter in an upscale Hollywood eatery.

It sounded too good to be true. I'd been hired as a busboy for 50 bucks to the party of the year: A closed-to-the-press, by-invitation-only, $5,000-a-couple fundraiser and backyard concert at Streisand's Malibu estate. Eat your heart out!

The last time I'd seen Streisand live was 22 years earlier in *Funny Girl* on Broadway. With my parents' blessings and the meager savings from a six-month stint as a bag boy at the local Safeway, my best buddy Sam and I *schlepped* by bus from downtown Denver to Penn Station, a decade before we knew from *schlepping*. Sam had been my Streisand guru; I, his eager student. Hey, some make a pilgrimage to the Promised Land, some to Our Lady Of Fatima; we went to the Winter Garden. Our parents told everyone, "Oh they're going to New York for the World's Fair." We did indeed, and I have no recollection. I do, however, recall going to the Winter Garden, like it was yesterday.

That was 1964 and this is 1986.

Dressed in borrowed, too-big tuxedo pants, my neighbor's half size too small shoes and my own clip-on bow tie, I depart for Malibu, rendezvous of the catering crew.

Following a map issued back at the restaurant, I arrive at the Bank of America on Pacific Coast Highway in Malibu at 3 PM.

"Hold it. Who are you with and for what party?"

This woman doesn't look like security; she's dressed in colorful silk cocktail party attire. I state my name, adding "I'm with Spago."

She checks her clipboard. "Park over there and check in with security."

Now, Security looks the part: a big, beefy mountain of a man. He wears reflective sunglasses, a very tight three-piece suit and leather driving gloves. He barks, "Name."

I find it on the long list of catering personnel and point. He records the hour and minute of my arrival, tosses me a button with my assigned number and instructs, "Don't lose it and don't take it off!"

My tendency is to salute, but before I have a chance a toothy teenager in a blazer embossed "Event Management" ushers me to a mini-van, jammed with other servers. The door is locked from the outside, and our driver (who looks like Security's brother, only meaner) re-checks our buttons, and we're off to Mesa Barbra, several miles and two security checkpoints away. The entrance is impressive and heavily guarded with guys holding rifles. We sign in. "Oh, isn't that nice," jokes a smart-alecky waiter, "Barbra's going to send us thank-you notes." Signs are posted: NO SMOKING. NO RECORDING EQUIPMENT. NO CAMERAS.

Much to my surprise, we are not strip searched.

Ambling up a gravel service road in little clusters, everyone dressed alike, we resemble either a flock of penguins or a new religious order. We gather at an opening off the very private tennis courts. This becomes home base; our makeshift kitchen. Our task is to turn the freshly astro-turfed courts into a formal dining patio.

Many of the staff are recruited for the day and, unlike myself, have little, if any, serving skills. Everyone is crazy about Streisand, but they don't have a clue about where butter knives go. It's instant camaraderie, the blind leading the extremely nearsighted.

Setting 50 tables with 500 place settings to Miss Manners' perfection with not enough room, too many flowers and napkins that must be folded to look like sea shells is no picnic, but we get the job done to "Event Management's" acceptance.

The guests begin arriving, also by vans, and we scurry up to a lawn where cocktails and appetizers are to be served.

This yard sprawls between two of the five homes on forty acres, nestled in the magnificent Malibu Canyon. All of the homes are radically different in period and style and the entire compound is called "The Ranch." Ain't nothin' ranchy about it. It looks like an over-manicured wealthy little community; complete with bubbling brooks, ornate bridges, gazebos, winding cobblestone walkways and anything else her little heart desires. The yard where we're serving appetizers is called the "Rose Garden." I know this because security guards keep squawking into their walkie-talkies, "Clyde here in the Rose Garden."

Even the illustrious guests are awed. "Dig this spread," crackles Jack Nicholson. "Amazing," Bruce Willis wheezes. "Unbelievable," Goldie Hawn giggles.

As I putter around serving little shish-kabobs in this come-to-life edition of *People*, there are certain surprises. A popular and affable Jack Nicholson looks older than I expect. Jane Fonda more beautiful. Bette Midler, Sally Field and Emmanuel Lewis even smaller. Chevy Chase looks bloated and talks too loud. And after all these years of grinning, Goldie Hawn's face looks like it hurts.

The invitation had specified "Hollywood Chic" as the attire and it finds various interpretations. Bruce Willis, in billowy black and white silk, looks like a gay priest (is that redundant?). Bette Midler, just moments from motherhood, takes the casual route in a sweatsuit and sneakers, while Rosanna Arquette wears an equestrian get-up, complete with bowler hat. But it's Carrie Leigh, on the arm of Hugh Hefner, who steals the show in a dress with no back and just enough front to cover her nipples. Although the crowd is of the political left, the rest of the guests mostly look like a bunch of Republicans: very neat, very tidy, very IBM.

This is not your everyday little backyard barbecue—no siree. And there are lots of no-no's. Signs are posted on the lawn: NO SMOKING. A fire marshal lingers in the background to make sure no one forgets. The houses are off limits and guards are posted everywhere to discourage wandering. There are no bathrooms, just a half dozen port-a-potties. Parked next to them is a stylish Winnebago with a woman guarding the door. As a famous face joins the lines at the stalls, she quietly invites them to use the more luxurious accommodations. No planes are allowed to fly over the property, as the FAA has restricted the air space. Talk about Barbra Power!

"So where is she?" several people mumble, looking around at the hostessless reception.

The waiter network passes word that she's hiding out in the large pink Victorian house, facing the lawn. Six guards at the entrance are a good indication that the grapevine is correct. I have this bizarre image of her at an upstairs window, watching us through binoculars.

Time for superstar suppertime. Everyone in the restaurant business knows the chaos and complete horror of serving more than 500 people simultaneously. Add to that . . . no kitchen, no running water and one inadequate food pick-up area, and you start to get the picture. And let's not forget that HBO is filming the after-dinner speeches for a TV special, so there are cables everywhere as well as hassled producer types. And the topper is that your customers are Walter Matthau, Eva Gabor, Ashford and Simpson and Senator what's-his-face, all milling about in an impromptu schmoozeathon.

Everyone seems to enjoy chef Wolfgang Puck's meal, but there are whispers that table #23 was never assigned a server and sat bewildered as everyone around them enjoyed tomato and goat cheese salad, veal chop with wild mushrooms, grilled veggies, raspberries, chocolate torte, coffee and a swirl of ice cream.

185

By the grace of God the meal finally ends and guests of honor—California Senator Alan Cranston and former Congressperson Barbara Jordan—give rousing anti-Reagan speeches to the roar of the liberal pinko crowd. Normally I would be cheering along, but I'm too busy eating up scraps of food I've managed to salvage. Somebody real snippy says, "That's against policy!" I stick my tongue out at her and she slithers away, appalled.

Speeches complete, the guests meander up to the small amphitheater built especially for the concert. Our once-elegant patio is left looking like downtown Lebanon.

"Now people, listen up." A supervisor claps his hands to get our dwindling attention. "First we have to clear the courts, then reset the lawn for coffee and cookies. And the faster we move people, the more of the concert we may be able to hear."

Hear? Hear! Not this busboy, babycakes. I am hungry, tired, my feet hurt, but I'm determined to see as well as hear.

I start to make my escape plans. Always the professional, I bus my section faster than the speed of sound. My final tray goes alongside dozens of others, waiting to be added to a heap of gourmet garbage large enough to feed the homeless of Hollywood, but we don't want to think about that. It's showtime!

I slip up a deserted winding staircase that leads to a maze of walkways and come face to face with an armed security guard in full uniform. Because of my uniform and the Spago apron, he just nods, continuing his rounds. I go the opposite direction, ending up at this all black-tiled swimming pool and patio like something out of a magazine. A screen door slides open and a thin voice asks, "Are you here for the dishes?" I stare at him nodding. He motions me inside. I gawk at the art deco palace as he points to the dining room table. "She didn't eat a bite," he whines. "The food went to the wrong house and by the time it got here, it was cold." I assume that "she" is Streisand, and I lift the untouched plate like a chalice.

So it's back down the stairs and across the patio, telling anyone who's interested "Here's her plate. It was cold. Didn't eat a bite."

Getting 500 movers-and-shakers port-a-pottied and seated is going to take some time. Robin Williams is opening for Streisand and word is he hasn't gone on yet. Most of the security force has moved to the theater area. I still have time. I sneak down the service road to a shack. Nobody's fool, I locate a jacket I'd stashed there earlier. The tie and apron get stuffed inside, and although I might not exactly be "Hollywood Chic," at least I don't resemble the catering crew.

On one side of this service road is a ravine; on the other, the property and a hill. I choose the hill, moving low, utilizing bushes, trees, shrubs, shadows and sure-footedness. I zig-zag up the hill, which crests at another service road. It comes from some other part of the property and descends right to the theater entrance, guarded like Fort Knox. Williams is just taking the stage as I start down the hill.

"Welcome to Temple Beth Malibu," he cracks. His voice bounces off the hills and open sky. The audience's roar is swallowed up by the valley and the earth.

Luckily, both HBO and Columbia Records are recording the concert and the hillside is conveniently littered with trailers, generators and mostly male crews. It's now or never. I walk towards the technicians, staying close enough to look included, but not so close as to blow my cover. One of the crew asks a guard a question. When he turns his back to answer, I move casually behind a light tower, my heart in overdrive.

I guess when you have five homes and several fireplaces in each, you need a lot of firewood, because there is a mountain of it stacked and bundled behind me. Like steps, it's easy to climb and ends at a foundation wall behind the top row of seats. Huge trees shield me, but through the branches I have a perfect view of the stage.

Another toothy teen is patrolling the hillside. He approaches. "Who are you with?" Twice his age, I'm not intimidated. "HBO," I say, sounding irritated. "Sorry," he shrugs. Anyway, these are only the $4,000 seats.

If you're a Streisand fan, what you won't get from the HBO special or the album is the chorus of crickets infesting my cozy little hill. When Streisand takes the stage she commands not only this oh-so-famous audience, but nature itself. I swear those crickets spend the next hour and a half playing The Pips to her Gladys Knight.

My time on the hill is magical, but short-lived. The concert ends with everyone standing, swaying in the aisles and trying to sing along to her shattering encore of "America the Beautiful."

It's back to reality. Struggling with my bow tie, I head back down. At this point, I figure if I get shot, it was worth it. I come around the light tower and step onto the road.

"Freeze. Stay right where you are. Don't move."

I don't. I'm standing perfectly still a few feet from a golf cart sort of thing, its motor purring. Guards start forming a wall around the cart, myself included, and a blinding light finds me. I figure it's adios when the light goes off and I realize I'm part of Streisand's inner security circle. In the sudden darkness and surrounded by guards she approaches, her shoulders covered with a towel. Not thinking, I compliment her on the concert. She seems surprised and says, "Thanks. It was O.K.?" I guarantee her it was just fine. She jumps on the cart and poof, she putters away, a platoon of guards following.

I look across the road and spot the horde of waiters and staff looking at me like I have crabs.

The audience is flooding out of the theater between us and onto the lawn for coffee and cookies. Some members of the audience go instead to the French Country style house where La Streisand is receiving her famous callers. I race around the area, avoiding Wolfgang and Company, find an empty coffee pot and fall in line behind Quincy Jones and Whitney Houston. Good company.

"Hey, you! Where do you think you're going?" snaps a guard about twice my size.

"Well. . . . I thought I'd pour coffee." I hold up my empty coffee pot to demonstrate.

Smarter than he looks, he barks, "No food or beverages allowed inside."

"Oh gosh. Well then we won't need this." I hold up the pot again. "Will we?"

"No . . . we . . . won't."

"We're gone."

And I am. Playing cat and mouse with Wolfgang and the catering staff, I once again put on my concert attire and hop on one of the first vans off the property. Whoopi Goldberg is nodding off in the seat in front of me. The van is going to the Malibu Community Club parking lot and I figure, how far can it be from the B of A lot? About fifteen miles north, it turns out.

"Excuse me, I'm from out of state and you'll never believe the idiotic thing I've done. Are you by any chance headed south on this Pacific Coast Highway Street here?"

"I am indeed. No problem. Hop in."

I'd never hopped into a mint green, mint condition '62 Bentley before. I could get used to it.

"Marvelous concert, don't you agree?" the driver inquires. "Well worth the price, wouldn't you say?"

"Oh indeed," I answer. "A bargain at twice the price."

SPARE US THE SCHMALTZ
Peter Watson
The London Observer, February 27, 1994

*T*here are few sights known to man that are more odious, more risible, than an auction house on the make, and in so doing being economical with the *actualité* in regard to the belongings of a rich customer. It must be one of the worst aspects of working in the auction trade—you have to call mutton lamb so often your taste buds must be shot to pieces.

Take, as an example, the Barbra Streisand 'collection' which goes on the block at Christie's in New York on Thursday and Friday. Now, there is no way that this lorry-load of litter could rate a perfect six from even the Russian judge, either for star quality or technical merit. But, Streisand being Streisand, the *actualité* has been *plié*-ed not a little.

What is, in fact, a perfectly respectable selection of art nouveau objects (in the main) is presented by Christie's—in a beribboned, boxed set of catalogues no less—as 'world class'. But this collection is no more world class than John Major is a world-class leader or Graeme Hick a world-class batsman. Christie's word appears about as reliable as that of the Bosnian Serbs.

There is also something risible about La Streisand's foreword in the snazzy catalogue. All she seems to care about is the *price* of her things—at least, this is what she keeps coming back to. We are told, twice, about her purchase of a Tiffany Cobweb lamp, for $55,000 (at a thrift shop in Manhattan, where she was 'amazed' at what you could find for $2). Whoever spends $55,000 on a lamp? she asked herself before promptly doing exactly that. She then records with glee that, three weeks later, a near-identical lamp sold for $150,000 and a year after that, for $400,000. She was, she says, *thrilled*. I'll bet. Christie's now has the gall to estimate the self-same lamp at $800,000–$1 million. To be fair to Ms. Streisand, her fruitwood and marquetry desk, designed by Julian Süssenbach in Berlin in 1901, her Frank Lloyd Wright casement window, her George Washington

189

Maher leaded glass table lamp, her Coüett jade clock and her Adam and Eve canvas by Tamara de Lempicka are all gorgeous. As are her eight lots of Louis Majorelle furniture, perhaps the finest part of the sale (Majorelle took over his father's furniture factory in Nancy, in 1879, at the age of 20).

But it was a mistake for Christie's to pepper its catalogue with photographs of Miss Streisand's homes (that is, the rooms in her houses). For these give the game away and highlight the enduring problem with art nouveau, which is that the whole, frequently, is considerably less than the sum of its parts.

If you fill a whole room with art nouveau, you end up with film sets, not homes. Art nouveau was designed to be looked at rather than lived in, or with. Nothing wrong with that, provided there is something else you can sit on, and relax in.

The perfect example of what I mean may be found in Paris, where the art nouveau designs for the metro stations stand out beautifully when surrounded by the straight, and more or less ugly, lines of the average streetscape. But if *all* Paris were art nouveau . . .

Funny Girl has gone for some eye-catching pieces, and very definitely has succeeded. But this has surely created rooms where everything competes with everything else, there is no background, only foreground, and no depth. As a whole, it just doesn't work. In her foreword in the catalogue, she asks 'where a person gets an eye'. Good question because, by and large, she doesn't have one. The objects she is selling are all 'obvious'. There is nothing subtle here. Everything—like so many of the roles she plays—hits you straight in the eye from the word go.

And here, maybe, is the crux of the matter. Ms. Streisand says she is selling because she wants to 'simplify' her life. 'I want only two houses, not seven.' Quite. But do we believe her? My bet is that, secretly, she has simply got tired of all these objects shouting at her, day in, day out. Buyers beware.

Incidentally, a catalogue note written by an anonymous Christie's hand shows how this otherwise British company has surrendered to that bland form of US airport-speak. 'Ms. Streisand's decision to sell her art nouveau and art deco collections at Christie's this March reflects a new desire to

190

simplify her lifestyle, and will enable collectors worldwide to share in her vision.

'Ms. Streisand has been an enthusiastic participant in this auction process, sharing with us her wisdom and ideas about the works she has so lovingly assembled.'

Apart from sounding as if the dear lady actually built the stuff herself, this makes me wonder if, when Christie's people go to bed at night, they say to their spouses: 'Would you like to be a participant in the love-making process?' I thought I would share that with you.

191

Barbra

the Icon

THE BARBRA STREISAND LITMUS TEST
Andy Tiemann (1995)

*J*f you were a teenage boy in Dallas, Texas, in the mid-1970s, and you wanted to make time with the prettiest girls in town, you needed three things: (1) an all-encompassing knowledge and adoration of the New Testament; (2) a membership in good standing with the Fellowship of Christian Athletes; and (3) the ability to converse intelligently about Barbra Streisand.

Now, the first two made perfect sense. The prize-winning adolescent beauties of that era and region were Southern Baptist girls who lived in North Dallas on either Meadow Lane or Boedeker Avenue. Their fathers were usually lawyers and their mothers were usually homemakers and they went to church three times a week. But why would Southern Baptist North Dallas teenage girls display such reverence for a Jewish New Yorker whose specialty was schmaltzy show tunes? It took me three years to figure it out.

The first Streisand fanatic I dated was Susan Jaross. Susan was adopted and was convinced that Streisand was her mother. Susan knew that she'd been born in New York in 1959, so technically it was conceivable, and that was enough for her, and since it was enough for Susan Jaross, by God it was enough for me, too. I was only 15 at the time, but I was intuitive enough to know that indulging the fantasies of the opposite sex is always a very good idea. So Susan and I would lie awake in our respective beds and talk on the phone for hours about the day when Barbra Streisand was going to knock on Susan's front door and say, "Hello, I'm your real mother. Come with me." And we'd talk about that moment in *The Way We Were* where Streisand tells Redford, "People are their principles," or we'd talk about the pregnant bride scene from *Funny Girl*, or about how sad it was that Streisand's nickname was Barbra Strident. To Susan, calling Barbra Streisand Barbra Strident was like calling God pompous: It missed the point of the whole damn thing altogether. I agreed with her because, frankly, I thought I might get lucky if I did. I didn't, so I got ants in my pants and moved on to an even bigger Streisand fan—Kathy Knippa.

Kathy Knippa was legendary. It was said that she could kiss like there was no tomorrow. It was also said that if she liked you, she would go so far as to rest her hand on your thigh for minutes at a time. This I had to see. Fortunately, God was on my side. On the morning of our first date, *A Star Is Born* opened at the Northpark Cinema. On the afternoon of our first date, an ice storm sailed over Oklahoma and into Dallas and then just sat down for a spell. When I picked Kathy up it was 12 degrees and I was elated because the heater in my Datsun B210 didn't work for nobody. This was going to be a night to remember.

Kathy started crying at the moment in *A Star Is Born* where Streisand spray-paints her name on Kristofferson's wall. She didn't have a handkerchief and neither did I, so Kathy began to burrow her face into my sweater to dry the tears. Kathy had one of those firm, perky, cheerleader noses, and I can still remember how exciting it felt as she rubbed it this way and that across my chest. Nothing in my life had ever been so arousing.

And then Kristofferson's drinking got worse. And then he shot at a helicopter. And then he drove a motorcycle off a stage and landed in a hospital. And Kathy cried and cried and burrowed and hugged and squeezed and my God it was sublime, and it was all because of Streisand and I couldn't have possibly been more grateful.

Then it hit me. I needed to be crying, too. Being a stouthearted preacher's kid, I wasn't much of a crier, but my older brother had told me what to do at a moment like this to ensure carnal victory. Carefully, I turned to my right and began surreptitiously yanking out all my nose hairs. This was about the time Streisand was belting out the finale, "Watch Me Now." Once all my nose hairs were plucked, I turned and looked straight at Kathy as my eyes gushed teardrops the size of Cleveland. Man, oh, man was she bowled over. Moses at the Red Sea was not even that beloved.

We rushed back to her place, staked out the couch, dimmed the lights, and just went to town. Then around midnight, Kathy placed her hand on my thigh. And left it there. Wow. This was mercy. This was as good as my life ever needed to get.

Eventually of course, not even Streisand could keep Kathy Knippa and me from being swallowed by the restlessness of youth, so it was on to

Debbie Hartfelder, who wasn't a fan of Streisand so much as a disciple. It was Hartfelder who unraveled the mystery of Streisand's appeal to these young Texas women.

Hartfelder and I were necking under the stars one night and it got a little heavy for her comfort, so she stopped and asked if we could talk for a while. Hartfelder never talked. She was so shy, people called her Deaf-Mute Debbie behind her back. Her wanting to talk was like Helen Keller spelling out w-a-t-e-r into Annie Sullivan's palm.

So I sat back and listened intently as she related the obvious: her father was a drunk and her mother was a doormat. And it suddenly hit me that Debbie's parents were a lot like Kathy's parents who were a lot like Susan's parents. In all 3 cases, the father was the bull, and the mother was the china shop, and the daughter was the storekeeper crouched in the corner hoping against hope that it would all end soon.

Then Hartfelder mentioned how Barbra Streisand would know what to do. If only Barbra Streisand were her mother, everything would be just fine because nobody but nobody would bully Streisand. No man would dare. If they did, she'd eat them alive and not even burp. Streisand was a real woman because Streisand knew how to take care of herself.

And that was her appeal. And that was her gift, her lovely, simple-hearted gift to these broken little girls of the Texas plains who had no choice but to watch their parents enact the same psychodrama night after night after night.

Seventeen years have passed since that moment with Hartfelder. I'm still single, and I still date, and I'm sure women still evaluate my suitability. But, of course, the rules have changed. Knowing all the lyrics to "Autumn Leaves" no longer helps me get the girl. What seems to matter now is what I do, and what I drive, and what I make.

So in a way, Streisand is useless to me now, at least in regards to women.

But I listen to her still. And when I do, I am still enchanted. But it's not because she's a genius. It's because she was once my comrade. She was once my comrade who came through for me again and again and again.

I'm sure I'll never meet Barbra Streisand. And I'm sure if I did, and I told her my tale, it wouldn't mean much to her.

But it damn sure means something to me.

STAR VS. BIOGRAPHER: THE FLAP & THE FURY
Richard Harrington
The Washington Post, January 19, 1986

THAT BARBRA STREISAND BOOK: A STIR IS BORN

*I*t's the unauthorized biographer versus the Star, and the fight is getting uglier by the day.

In the near corner, Shaun Considine, author of the recently released "Barbra Streisand: The Woman, The Myth, The Music." The Delacorte book charts Streisand's ascension to megastardom, and Considine, the jacket claims, "has gotten to the people who were there—those who worked with her, helped her, watched her, hurt her, loved her, hated her—*and they have talked.*"

In the far corner, Streisand and her longtime press agent, Lee Solters, who has sent form letters to everyone quoted in Considine's book asking if the quotes are accurate. In some cases, the answer has been no.

"This is just another one of those paste-up biographers trying to latch on to the coattails of someone in the limelight hoping for instant notoriety and instant wealth," raged Streisand (who rarely talks to the press and declined to be interviewed for this story) in a statement released by Solters. "Without any conscience this writer fills this book with outrageous gossip deceptively presented as fact, conversations that are invented between people never spoken to and statements maliciously taken out of context."

"It's terrific publicity," said Considine, who denies Streisand's charges. The first printing has already sold out, and a second edition is being rushed into bookstores.

Shaun Considine is a well-traveled journalist whose articles have appeared in *People* and *The New York Times.* His book was three years in the making. Published in November, it depicts Streisand as a woman and artist loved by millions but "despised" by others for being "cool and aloof, a woman admittedly with talent but with no sincerity and little integrity."

198

It further casts the temperamental star as a control freak who has claimed sole credit for songs she didn't write alone (her alleged collaborators have said she deserves sole credit), and who has deceived her fans about the creative process behind several albums; a penny pincher who used to stiff New York cab drivers and recycle her Christmas cards; an egocentric actress who had affairs with leading men Ryan O'Neal and Omar Sharif while married to Elliot Gould.

There is also much reporting about Streisand's business dealings, particularly with her record company, Columbia. Through it all, the Streisand portrayed by Considine is definitely *not* a Funny Lady.

Streisand refused to be interviewed for the biography, despite 15 months of requests made through Lee Solters. "I was told she was going to talk," says Considine. "I told Lee there were quite a few provocative things in the book. I tried to make it fair and balanced, even delayed it trying to get her cooperation. Nothing ever happened and then the book came out and Barbra hit the roof."

In December, Solters sent form letters to every one of the several hundred people quoted in the book (even those quoted favorably), with photocopied, marked passages attached. The letters asked whether Considine had actually talked to them, whether they were quoted correctly and whether the quotes attributed to them had been extracted from other interviews without crediting the sources.

"People called me and told me about the letters," Considine reports. "Barbra personally called a lot of these people, who in turn called me. She's furious that I got to so many people. She's annoyed that I found out the details of her affairs, annoyed about the stories of her being so frugal, annoyed that I spoke about the deception on certain albums like 'Classical Barbra,' where I said it took six months of secret editing to splice it together . . . a *lot* of things. Solters is under the gun from Barbra, that's for sure."

Solters denies that, saying the letter campaign was his idea. Streisand, he insists, didn't even know about it. "I've been her publicist for 25 years," says Solters, who also handles Frank Sinatra and Dolly Parton, among others. "Any time I read or hear something that I doubt or question about a client, I always check the veracity so that in the interest of accuracy, I can make a statement or correct a false statement."

"I don't know what [Solters] is planning to do with the letters," Considine says, though such information-gathering is often a prelude to a lawsuit. "He's also violating my copyright by Xeroxing passages from the book, if I wanted to get picky . . .

"When this book was started, it was just going to be a chronicle of the music years. But so many things came up. One person would say, why don't you call so and so, and one thing led to another." Considine also placed an ad in *The New York Times Book Review* "for anyone who had ever worked with her. Well, the mail I got. *Everybody's* got a Barbra Streisand story."

Solters, who accuses Considine of a "paste and scissors" job, says many of those stories have been told elsewhere to other interviewers. Solters says he's been swamped with letters from celebrities who said they never spoke with Considine, including Jane Fonda, Harold Arlen, Sydney Pollack, Barry Gibb, Ray Stark, Jule Styne, Carol Burnett and Ryan O'Neal (who, according to Solters, wrote that "this guy is hokum, I've never spoken to him . . . none of those words are mine").

While Solters marshals his letters, Considine marshals his responses. Many of those quotes, he points out, *are* from other sources and most of the people named by Solters are not listed in his acknowledgments. "Anyone that's in the acknowledgments, I spoke to, I interviewed. I have the names, dates, notes, letters, tapes.

"The quotes from Jane Fonda were taken from a tape honoring Barbra that I have. How could she deny it? Then Bella Abzug denied her quote and it was in her autobiography! There's nothing out of context, and I tried to list everybody that I took quotes from."

Says Solters: "Of course, there's some semblance [of reality], but when I went through that book—and I've been with her for 25 years—there were facts that kept popping out of the page that flashed TILT. My own personal, professional opinion? TRASH."

EVERGREEN

The star's opinion? "This book," Streisand's statement reads, "is overwhelmingly filled with inaccuracies and blatant distortions from its front cover where the photograph is used without permission, down to the last page where he quotes a supposed friend of mine speaking about my current finances—the 'friend' being someone I have not seen or spoken to in 25 years."

Streisand seems to have been particularly upset by Considine's suggestion that she did not write "Evergreen"—her Oscar-winning song—alone, but with the uncredited help of singer-songwriter Rupert Holmes.

"In his desperate need to create sensationalism for publicity," she writes, Considine "even stoops as low as to suggest that I only wrote part of the melody for 'Evergreen,' which is as ludicrous as saying I didn't sing in 'Funny Girl,' but he never asked Rupert Holmes, whom he alludes to having written the melody with me."

Considine says he heard the story from Bruce Lundvall, who was at the time the president of CBS Records, and tried to get it confirmed by Holmes. Considine said he set up an interview, but that Holmes canceled at the last minute and thereafter failed to return his phone calls. "The information came from Norman Kurtz, his attorney, who said there was collaboration on 'Evergreen.' "

Lundvall, now president of Manhattan Records, says he told Considine "that I had heard that Rupert Holmes had written or co-written the song. I don't remember who told me this and I don't know to this day whether he had anything to do with the song. It was a rumor, not fact, and I never told him that I had inside knowledge that she did not write it."

Lee Phillips of Manatt, Phelps, Rothenberg, Tunney and Phillips, Streisand's law firm, says he also has a signed statement from Ettore Stratta saying he had nothing to do with co-writing another disputed song, "Ma Premiere Chanson."

According to Considine, after the book came out, Streisand's lawyers "wanted corrections on that and I refused . . . She called up Ettore Stratta, who told me about it, and he denied ever saying it. But I have the whole thing on tape." People are trying to cover themselves, he says. "This is a very strong lady." Christopher Goff, Delacorte's lawyer, would only say that, "the matter has been under discussion by attorneys for Delacorte and attorneys for Barbra Streisand."

Says Considine's editor, Chuck Adams: "All nonfiction books, especially about living people, are put through very close scrutiny and are looked at by our lawyers . . . Everything that was possibly controversial, and I mean *everything,* was carefully looked at and documented." Considine remembers that there were about 300 points of discussion with Delacorte.

In December, the book was serialized in the New York *Daily News*— but not before some conversations with Solters. "The thrust of what he said was 'You should be very careful running this book because Barbra has her lawyers on,' " says Anthea Disney, the *Daily News'* assistant features editor. "He said there were several things she was concerned about. We assumed they would be things like her personality being revealed through the way she treated her ex-husband, things like that."

But it was the authorship questions that arose, Disney says. "It was suggested to us by Solters that litigation would follow if we brought up the fact that there was a question that she's written these songs." Solters says he never mentioned lawyers.

The unusual thing, Disney says, is that top-level press agents like Solters "don't return calls under normal circumstances . . . but he was on the phone damn quick about those two songs. Suddenly he's calling us back like crazy, leaving urgent messages. I nearly fell off my chair." The *Daily News* ended up not running the section in question, though Disney says "it wasn't a decision made on Lee Solters' say-so. We were looking for Barbra the Woman, and whether she wrote the songs was neither here nor there."

Meanwhile, Streisand's record company has been trying to distance itself from the book.

"CBS did not help, assist or cooperate in any way," says Bob Altshuler, vice president for press and public affairs for CBS Group. "We're doing our best to ignore it." In fact, CBS wrote a letter to Delacorte protesting Considine's acknowledgments to several CBS employees including Altshuler, who says he has "no memory whatsoever" of having talked to Considine. The author says he has the conversation on tape.

"From what I have read, a lot of the information he collected is just wrong, pure speculation," says Altshuler. "If individuals talked to him on their own, they were not representing CBS Records or Columbia in any way."

Two of the CBS employees quoted in the book by name, art directors

Bob Berg and Virginia Team, lost their jobs in December, in part of an early retirement and job reclassification austerity program involving 38 employees. "Absolutely no connection whatsoever," says Altshuler. "It was completely coincidental."

"I got upset when I heard about that and called them," Considine says, "and they said they didn't think it had anything to do with that BUT . . ."

"I thought about it," Team says from Nashville, adding that she wasn't sure she knew what Considine was writing when she talked to him. "I wish to hell I'd kept my mouth shut, but whether there's any connection, I don't know."

Berg, a 24-year CBS employee, confirms it was "a general layoff. I was quoted correctly," he adds. "I can't speak to the stuff I don't know about, but certainly the stuff that I do know about is accurate."

ON A CLEAR DAY, YOU CAN SUE FOREVER

"I don't know what he's planning," Considine says of Solters and his letter campaign.

"We have virtually found inaccuracies on every page, if not every paragraph," says Streisand's attorney, Lee Phillips. "Obviously, since I'm a lawyer and am involved, we're considering what should or shouldn't be done, but no decision has been reached. There are various possible rights and remedies and they are all being investigated."

There's no word yet on whether New York cab drivers are considering a class action suit over Streisand's alleged past penny pinching.

Meanwhile, both sides continue to muster their facts and forces, getting testimonials to the accuracy or inaccuracy of quotations, appraisals of whether contexts are correct or misleading.

"As for me, I refuse to be intimidated," says Considine, who says he has two file cabinets stuffed with documentation.

Streisand, he added—getting in a late, but certainly not the last, shot—"should see what I've left out. If Lee Solters doesn't let up, she's going to have it in the paperback."

1993—The Post Office in Grenada issued a 90-cent postage stamp honoring Barbra Streisand. Unfortunately, the first issue of 100,000 stamps was misprinted, naming "Barbara" Streisand.

"Grenada is a small country with a small population," said a representative of the Grenada Post Office. "The mistake will have to stand."

Tony Rizzo: "THE GREATEST VOICE I'VE EVER KNOWN"

Karen Moline

Excerpted from *Streisand Through the Lens,* by Karen Moline, 1982

A Hollywood photographer, Tony Rizzo is a transplanted New Yorker who began shooting stills of the stars when he was eleven and sold his first picture when he was fourteen. His photographs have appeared in NEWSWEEK, TIME, TV GUIDE, US, PEOPLE, PHOTOPLAY, and LADIES' HOME JOURNAL, as well as the LONDON SUNDAY MIRROR and other foreign publications. A frequent talk-show guest, Tony has also been a staff writer and photographer for SOAP OPERA DIGEST for the past five years, and a former columnist/writer for PHOTOPLAY.

KAREN MOLINE:

How did your career as a photographer begin?

TONY RIZZO:

When I was eleven years old, I used to hang out at the candy store on Second Avenue and 12th Street. Right next door was the Phoenix Theater (now Entermedia), a very prominent off-Broadway theater. I met Carol Burnett there—she was playing *Once Upon A Mattress.* And I'd go up to Studio 50 to see her on *The Garry Moore Show.* She would get me her house seats. We'd go out for a Coke between the dress rehearsal and the taping, and she'd cue me for the response—audiences need to be led!—there were no overhead cues for laughter, only applause. Well, one night, during the opening number of *Garry Moore*, all the cast and stars came riding out on a golf cart, including Robert Goulet and Barbra Streisand. She looked very unusual to be a star. We still didn't know who she was. She did her first number standing in a window in a set of a house, singing "When the Sun Comes Out." When she finished, the audience gave her a standing ovation for twenty minutes. In the second half, she sang "Happy Days." Later, they said that she was appearing in *I Can Get It For You Wholesale,* so I left the audience and ran up to the Shubert Theater. I snuck in for the second half (which is when she had her big number as Miss

Marmelstein). I fell in love with her immediately. At that time, I used to run around looking for stars. I'll tell you a little-known fact: Carol Burnett was offered *Funny Girl* first. She turned it down and suggested Barbra Streisand.

Through Carol Burnett I met all these stars, and I decided I had to have pictures of them. I bought a Brownie Starflash. I was taking pictures all the time. I started with black and white and went to color. I got to meet all these people: I'd go to the hotels where they were staying and I'd call them up on the house phones and say, "Hello, Miss Garland, this is a fan of yours and I'd like to know when you are coming down so I can get your autograph." And she'd say, "Oh, about nine o'clock." And she'd come down at eleven. She was always late.

What was the first picture you took of Barbra?

I saw her backstage and said, "Can I take your picture?" and she said, "Oh, I look terrible," but I took it anyway. It was so bad I threw it out. One day in the doorway of Korvettes on Fifth Avenue, she was there with Elliot Gould, and she introduced him to me as "My fiancé." I called up Earl Wilson at the *Post* and he ran it in his column. Anyway, when I was fourteen, my parents thought it was sick that I was chasing after movie stars. They said, "You want to be an actor, we'll give you acting lessons, but taking pictures is disgusting." So they cut my allowance. Four dollars a week. I needed the money, so I went to all the movie magazines, and the last one I called, *Motion Picture* magazine, bought my first photograph. A full-page in color. They paid $75, which was a lot of money in 1962.

When I was seventeen, I made my first trip to California for the Academy Awards for *TV/Radio Mirror* magazine, and the following year I covered the Emmy Awards. I decided to move to California in 1968—I was nineteen.

And on October 17, 1968—I remember that date well—I was covering the discotheques. I wasn't doing well at all; I was starving as a matter of fact. But even though I went to press events where there was plenty of food, I never ate because the press corps had such a bad reputation for that. You never saw a photo of me with a fork in my mouth! So I was shooting a screening of a Steve McQueen movie. Barbra Streisand and Elliot Gould were there with Terry Leff and Abbe Lane. As they were leaving, Barbra kept hiding her face, and Elliot was dragging her away. Three other photographers and myself were following them, trying to get a shot. Barbra kept saying, "You have enough! You have enough!"—even though we didn't have anything at all. And I said, "If you had been polite and stopped for us, we wouldn't have to bother you now." Elliot lunged forward and grabbed the chain of my camera and began to choke me. He was choking me with the chain of my own camera. He said, "I'll break your camera, you son-of-a-bitch!!" And I said, "Watch your mouth, there are ladies present." He then threw me down in the gutter, against a parked car. As a result, I dislocated my shoulder and did damage to my back and neck. I still can't hold a camera steady without a tripod. I was out of work for three months. I filed suit and it got to court three years later. That was June of 1971. Gould was found guilty on all three charges of battery. And the judge—while Gould was on the witness stand—asked him for his autograph. Right *after* that, the judge pronounced him guilty. I was awarded $6,501 in damages. As we were walking out of court, Gould said to me, "I hope you can go far on that."

He was being sarcastic?

He told reporters, "This is funnier than all my movies." They asked him if he thought it was fair. His lawyer dragged him away before he could say anything.

You must have been happy about the verdict.

Of course I was happy. I won. Now all the other members of the press corps can take pictures without being bullied by the actors. Once we were out of court, Elliot Gould walked over to me. I said, "I hope you understand it's a matter of precedent and principle," and I extended my hand. He said, "I hope you know why I can't do that." And he walked away, over to the camera crews. He told them, "The joke's on him. I don't have the money." That was broadcast on the news and I got a check two days later. Now he's always nice to me if we see each other.

You saw him often after that?

The next time I saw him was about a year later. I was in a little restaurant, and I was trying to get out of the place, but he was sitting at a table near the doorway. I saw him there, and was hoping he'd finish before I did. But I had an appointment, and had to leave, so I went to the cash register, and I heard him say to the man with him, "Hey, ain't that the Rizzi character?"

He called you Rizzi?

Yes, and I thought, Oh God, what do I do—should I go out the front door or look for the back door. But I looked him right in the eye and said, "Hi, how you doing," and walked out the door. The next time I saw him was about six months later at a screening of *Lenny*, in Westwood. Though the snack bar was closed, I was standing near it, and I heard someone come in behind me and say, "It's that guy who wins lawsuits against me." I turned around, and there was Elliot Gould facing me, with his elbow on the counter, leaning on his knuckles, you know, and he smiled at me. I said, "How you doin', Elliot," and turned and walked away. The next time was at a party in Beverly Hills. I walked in, and was standing on this sort-of elevated platform and he came racing toward me. Everybody thought he was going to hit me, but he said, "How ya doing!" He shook my hand; he was really friendly.

Do you think he acted that way because there were so many other people around?

No, I think he wanted to get it over, something of the past. One time, Barbra had approval of a cover for *Cosmopolitan* magazine, and they had selected one of my pictures, from *Funny Girl*. When she found out who the photographer was, she had it pulled. That was hard. It would have been a great credit to have a *Cosmo* cover.

Did the incident hurt your business because people saw you as a litigious photographer, or did they feel sorry for you?

They made fun of me for years. "Oh there he is—anybody hit you up this week? Ha ha ha." That was one of the big points of the trial. I was embarrassed publicly. It was in all the trade papers; on the front page of the *Hollywood Reporter:* "Tony Rizzo Wins Suit With Gould." Streisand, after the first day in court, was removed from the suit because she didn't actually hit me.

Did she remember you as the person who used to hang out and be a big fan?

I don't think she paid enough attention to remember. You know, I was thinking, very carefully, about giving you a statement about why Streisand acts the way she does in public. And I came to a very good conclusion. On *Funny Girl*, Streisand's first movie, she was reported to have ten or twelve cinematographers fired, because she had to be photographed a certain way, to her liking.

Her left side?

Well, one side is for comedy, and one side is for everything else. When she goes out to a public event, she wants to minimize the amount of still pictures taken of her that she has no control over. So, she hides. Or people date her to protect her. After Elliot Gould, Ryan O'Neal got into a scuffle with photographers, Jon Peters scuffled with photographers. Anyone she's ever gone out with has had to *protect* her. From what, I don't know. Having her picture taken? And I think it's because she feels that she can't control what she is going to look like so she doesn't want *anything* taken. In the sense of promotion—she's protected and hidden and guarded—it works to her advantage.

I wonder if she's basically a nice person.

I don't know her as a person; I only know her as a talent. And I only know her as a lady on the run.

Does how you feel about her talent override what you feel about her as a person?

Let's put it this way. I feel flattered that Barbra Streisand won't speak to me. It means she had to speak to me once. It's a distinction!

Most photographers see her as way up there on a pedestal, unapproachable, but you've had this unfortunate kind of direct contact with her.

I think she's probably the greatest talent of all times. I feel very lucky to have photographs of her as I do. But as a person, I think she must be

209

terribly unhappy, because she finds herself in a kind of prison—a minimum security prison where she is isolated from the rest of the world. She cannot walk among the people. She would not be comfortable walking among the people. And when she goes out in public it's an ordeal for her. And I sympathize with her. I really feel sorry for her. I mean, in a sense it's over-paranoia. One of my greatest dreams when I was younger and hoping to be an actor, was to work with Barbra Streisand, but I know now it will never happen. So . . . I just have a tremendous respect for her talent and her and I feel very sad about how her life has gone.

How has Barbra's appearance changed over the years?

When I saw Barbra Streisand in Shubert Alley when she was doing *Wholesale,* she used to be led around by her mother and Barbra used to wear a bun on top of her head, and very drab, second-hand clothes. Then when she did *Funny Girl,* she used to dress in jeans and motorcycle jackets. Now her looks are more classic. She's got more money and more control, and more taste. She dresses much nicer—she always dresses very well—although people thought that what she wore the year that she won the Oscar was godawful!

What do you consider to be her most outstanding characteristic?

Her voice.

Anything physical?

Her nose. That goes without saying, doesn't it? I've always been fascinated by her nose, because I have a big nose myself. But I have been fascinated by the way her nose has changed over the years.

Has it really changed?

Look at her early pictures and look at her most recent pictures, and you can tell the difference. When I was a guest on *The Steve Allen Show* in 1971, I showed pictures of the stars. And when I showed early Streisand and more recent Streisand, they made me go back and forth. They commented on how she looks as though she's had a nose job.

Have you ever noticed her fingernails?

She has very, very long fingernails. I would not want to be caught in an alley with her. That reminds me of a story. She went to a screening of *Willy Wonka and the Chocolate Factory,* and she brought her son Jason along. When she was leaving she came out the back way and all the photographers got at the foot of the staircase where she had to go down. But I went onto a service porch, which was off to her side. I got pictures of her from the back with all the other photographers as a backdrop. And at one point she turned around and said to her son Jason, "Stick out your tongue at the awful man." He turned around and stuck out his tongue at me.

That's terrible! She must have given you a complex.

No, it rolls off my back. But you know, Streisand is Streisand, and having her kid stick his tongue out at me is better than nothing at all. Shooting Barbra is always exciting. It was always a challenge when you came into contact with her because you knew you were going to get a run for your money. And you may quote me on that one.

For Streisand fans, real or fictional, the Las Vegas concerts are worth paying a bundle for.

*M*ike Myers says that Linda Richman, his character from the "Coffee Talk" skits on "Saturday Night Live," is all "farklempt," about seeing Barbra Streisand's first full-fledged commercial concert since 1966.

"I'm going to see Barbra," the actor said in his character's trademark Long Island accent. "I can't believe it!"

He was speaking to Jay Leno on the "Tonight" show recently, explaining that he—and in effect Mrs. Richman, a notorious Streisand fan—would attend one of the two New Year's concerts in Las Vegas.

"She's getting all tootsed up," Mr. Myers said of his alter ego, who once had a surprise visit from the singer on the "Coffee Talk" set. "I think this is the pinnacle of her life."

Indeed, for those like Linda, to whom Barbra is "like butter," the shows, on New Year's Eve and New Year's Day, are *the* events. And with the high prices that people are paying for tickets, the concerts had better be the pinnacle of something.

There were 12,805 tickets made available to the general public in November for each show at the 15,200 seat MGM Grand Garden arena, part of a new $1 billion complex that opened on Dec. 18. The complex includes the world's largest hotel, a casino and a theme park. Frank Sinatra will also be playing the MGM Grand those same nights—in a smaller theater.

The Streisand tickets sold out instantly, despite prices of $50 to $1,000. In mid-December, 600 more tickets to the two shows were released, most of them for $1,000 seats.

Now, the only tickets for sale are in the hands of scalpers and ticket

212

brokers. The $1,000 seats have been going for nearly $2,000 at ticket agencies.

Although the concert is shaping up as a prime event for Los Angeles and New York show-business types, Washington's two biggest stars won't be in the audience.

"It's not on the President and Mrs. Clinton's schedule," said Neel Lattimore, the deputy press secretary to the First Lady. President Clinton already saw Ms. Streisand perform this year—was serenaded by her, even—at his inauguration festivities.

But others are scrambling to be part of the anticipated magic in the new MGM Grand Garden.

"The calls we get are concentrated from L.A., and we've gotten a number of calls from Florida and New York," said Lance Keller, the general manager of Murray's Tickets in Los Angeles. Most of the ticket buyers seem to be middle-aged, he added, and share two common traits:

"They're big fans of Barbra and they've got some disposable income. What it costs is secondary."

A publicity executive from a major Hollywood studio who said she didn't want colleagues to know she was spending so much money on the concert nevertheless added that she was happy to spend $2,000 for a pair of tickets—not to mention the cost of air fare and a hotel room.

Cathy Rand, a travel agent who lives in Queens, says she regrets that she can't go to Las Vegas for the show.

"I wish I'd booked myself," she said. "It's exciting. I'm a big fan."

She said that a friend of her daughter has a ticket and that "we're all envious of him."

The brokers' ticket prices "will probably cap out at $3,000," said Mr. Keller in Los Angeles, adding that he expects to sell about 100 of the most expensive seats. By contrast, a 50-yard-line seat at the Super Bowl goes for $2,500, tops, he said.

To sell out the concerts, all the MGM Grand had to do was advertise in big-city newspapers in the United States. The hotel got calls from all 50 states, and many from Canada and England, even though there was no advertising in those countries, Richard Sturm, the MGM Grand's senior vice president of marketing and entertainment, said.

Forget about finding a bargain for the concerts. The cheapest Streisand tickets available through agents will cost up to $500, Mr. Keller said. "I can't think of another face value of $1,000 for a concert ticket," he added.

Dick Guttman, Ms. Streisand's publicity agent, said: "She's built up demand. She's appeared at other events, but in every case they were to raise money for some charity or social issue."

Ticket sellers are apparently not the only people raking in the money. Trade publications have reported that Ms. Streisand is getting as much as $20 million for the two performances; neither Mr. Guttman nor the hotel's management would disclose a figure.

Mr. Sturm would not even say whether the hotel would turn a profit on the concerts—or if they would be written off as a promotional expense.

To die-hard fans, the concerts are the chance of a lifetime, said Richard Simmons, the television fitness and diet guru who has been a Streisand fan since 1965, when as a teen-ager he "fell in love with her."

"She was like the little skinny kid that people made fun of, and I was the little fat kid that people made fun of," said Mr. Simmons, who over the years has collected about 1,500 photographs of Ms. Streisand.

"It's like so exciting to me," he said of seeing Ms. Streisand perform. "I send her flowers. I send her gifts. I send her cards. She's always written me nice letters back, and now I get this honor. Only 30,000 people in the whole world will be in on this.

"Her voice, her sense of humor, her beauty—let's face it: I'd take up tennis to meet her."

YOU KNOW YOU'RE IN LOVE WITH BARBRA STREISAND WHEN . . .

from *Just Like Buttah* fanzine, September 1994

You know you're in love with Barbra Streisand when . . .

. . . you have an uncontrollable urge to say "Hello, Gorgeous" every time you pass a mirror.

. . . you name your two cats Dolly and Levi.

. . . people you work with bring you newspaper clippings of anything to do with Barbra Streisand, and it's only your first week on the job.

. . . you receive a crystal picture frame as a wedding gift that says "One Love That Is Shared By Two," and you put a picture of Barbra in it.

—Bill from New York

216

. . . you name your twin sons Hubbell and Avigdor.

. . . you totally accepted Jason as a football player in "The Prince of Tides."

. . . you gave a speech in college about Barbra's album covers which was supposed to be five minutes long but you went on for over 15 minutes holding each one of them up in class and explaining their significance to the world.

. . . you wish your 14-minute version of "Enough Is Enough" were longer.

—Francis from Colorado

. . . you convince your younger sister to play "Love With All the Trimmings" at her wedding.

. . . you trick family and friends into seeing "Yentl" by convincing them it was a sequel to "Fiddler on the Roof."

. . . you teach French by making your students listen to "Je m'Appelle Barbra."

. . . you wish Katie and Hubbell would get back together.

. . . you think Barbra could run the country better than Bill or Hillary.

—Tom from Texas

217

A LOOK AT HER FIRST 100 DAYS IN OFFICE.

Because Stranger Things Have Happened.

*T*he 100th day of the Streisand administration dawned bright and clear, symbolic of the optimism and confidence that have pervaded the nation since her inauguration a little more than three months ago. Confounding the critics who doubted that the award-winning performer/visionary could succeed in Washington, President Streisand has turned the town on its head.

From the outset, the reputedly egotistical Streisand disarmed dubious observers with her self-effacing manner. "I was wrong long ago," she said in her inaugural address. "People who need people aren't lucky. People who need entitlement programs are lucky, because we're not cutting a penny from their grants."

Then, sounding her theme of sacrifice and civic renewal, the new president recalled the labors of the pioneers who built the nation. "Could it be that it was all so simple then, or has time rewritten every line? If we had the chance to do it all again, tell me, would we? Could we?"

Stirred by this implicit challenge, the public warmly responded to her call to national service. "You and I must make each night a first, every day a beginning," she intoned, the very image—in her gray Donna Karan suit cut to reveal a clinging peach camisole—of feminine power. Our freedoms, she said, "warm and excite us, for we have the brightest system of checks and balances."

Afterward, responding to cries for an encore, she rescheduled until that evening's MTV party the dramatic reading of "America the Beautiful" by

Andre Agassi, and instead brought Neil Diamond out of the grandstand for a duet of their 1978 hit "You Don't Bring Me Flowers."

In February, Streisand delighted the public with a series of unannounced forays into shopping malls to take the nation's pulse. Often she traveled in disguise, usually that of a young rabbinical student. In March, the president flew to Sarajevo, where she negotiated an end to the still-festering Balkan situation. Experienced diplomats were awestruck by her style. "She has outdone me," Henry Kissinger told NBC. "Could I have greeted Slobodan Milosevic by saying, 'Hello, gorgeous'? Could I have flicked my perfectly manicured fingernails at his temples and said, 'In my country, powerful men seldom have such thick hair'? I think not."

Yet she was not all sweetness. Applying what she called her "studio strategy," Streisand distracted Milosevic with complaints about her accommodations, her dining arrangements, and the way his premier pronounced her name ("Not Strei-SEND, Strei-SAND!" she told the confused, non-English speaking official). Eventually, Milosevic became so unnerved that he withdrew Serbian troops to pre-1992 borders and voluntarily turned himself into the United Nations War Crimes Tribunal.

Though the achievement was saluted, the president is said to have felt slighted. Longtime admirer Shirley MacLaine proposed that the Academy of Motion Picture Arts and Sciences present Streisand with a special Oscar for her work. When officials declined, the president was unhappy. "What?" she reportedly fumed. "Did this treaty negotiate itself?"

In April, Streisand rammed through Congress an economic program that both cut the deficit and generated business activity. The turning point came at a meeting when she secured the support of Senate Minority leader Bob Dole.

"It was quite a moment," recalled Dole. "I was sitting in the Oval Office, and she just looked at me and said, 'What's really wrong, Bobby? Why are you really so mean?' Well, I just became overcome. I saw her lustrous hair, her shapely legs, and I started thinking of the warmth I felt from her when I started giving football tips to her son. I found myself blurting out a long-forgotten memory of the night thieves broke into my home and began raping everyone until my brother shot them. Suddenly I understood why I was so mean, and I dropped my opposition. Later, my wife told me I was remembering some damn video she was watching when I was dozing on the couch. But the economy's okay, so what the hell."

Breaking after the arduous opening pace for a ski vacation in Sun Valley (still boycotting Aspen, Streisand calls herself "president of forty-nine states"), she was asked what she would address next. "All I want is for America to be a haven where everybody feels really fabulous," she replied. "After that, we'll talk about a second term."

220

THE WAY SHE WAS
Camille Paglia
The New Republic, July 1994

*O*n June 20, at Madison Square Garden, Barbra Streisand gave her first live performance in New York City in twenty-seven years. As a public figure, she had been absent from her hometown longer than Odysseus. It was here that she rose from homely Flatbush teen to kooky Greenwich Village chanteuse and then to toast of Broadway.

Transplanted to Los Angeles, Streisand attacked and conquered the world of movies without ever being accepted by the Hollywood establishment. Edgy, suspicious and dogged by stage fright, she became the Kubla Khan of her own entertainment empire. As producer, director and star, she absorbed all roles and crushed the identities of co-workers and subordinates to fulfill her exotic, florid personal vision. She craved fame but fled personal contact with her vast audience.

At the Garden, Streisand was scarcely alone—she was accompanied by Marvin Hamlisch, a sixty-four-piece orchestra and an eleven-piece suite of ornate antique furniture to lounge on—but she seemed as pure and fragile as crystal, broken pieces of which glittered on her white gown. After greeting her with a standing ovation, the audience held its breath. Did Streisand still have it? Who could function under such pressure?

The last time I had seen Streisand live was in 1964, when I was an avid 17-year-old fan and she was a smash hit as Fanny Brice in *Funny Girl* and still an endearing, tremulous ingenue. Since then she has become a major diva, with the volatile temperament and flair for melodrama of legendary opera stars. After an avant-garde cabaret start, her tastes went mainstream. Early Streisand was sophisticated and satirical; midcareer Streisand was overstated and bourgeois. With no feeling for rock music, the central expression of her generation, she might well have become irrelevant, except for her constant presence in movies of widely ranging quality.

The Garden audience was heavily baby boomer. In many ways, it was a homecoming. The rich range of New York Jewish society turned out in force. Those who had been in high school or college at her debut were now visibly prosperous professionals with college-age children of their own. Everywhere I was happily jostled by mesmerizingly powerful women, from the old-style Yiddish-inflected dowagers, barreling down the aisles like tanks, to the assimilationist era's tanned, vivacious, sylphlike princesses, whom Ali MacGraw skillfully played in *Goodbye, Columbus.* Matriarchal Jewish culture, from which Streisand sprang, never needed feminism to liberate its raucously outspoken women. The other major segment of the audience was gay men, Streisand's original hard-core fans. They circulated as discreet duos, with cropped hair and trim physiques, and in matching outfits, either beige summer suits or black tuxedo jackets over white T-shirts.

Before the show everyone was forced through metal detectors and a handbag inspection, a relic of Streisand's fear, at her 1967 Central Park concert, of being assassinated by the PLO over her support of Israel. Inside, vendors hawked $20 programs. ("It will be worth money!" barked a zaftig mother to her skeptical daughter), $25 T-shirts, $50 cotton throws, $60 ties and $400 "official tour jackets." All bore the Streisand image, eyes or fancy, feminine "B" logo, which looked suspiciously like the opulent, half-exposed Streisand breasts on the program cover. Inflation was also the theme of the ticket prices ($50 to $350), which one was invited to forget by sampling champagne and strawberries, served for a price alongside the arena's usual hot dogs and fries. Having extorted a river of cash from the crowd, Streisand had set herself up for failed expectations. The nervous quiet was shattered by a grandiose orchestral medley of her hits, with bursts of violins and trumpets. Streisand appeared in a blaze of white light and, with simple dignity, began to sing. It was as if she were resuming a conversation interrupted yesterday. She was flawless. Tears flowed freely in the audience. No tribute seemed too high for the exquisite quality of tone, rhythm, dynamics, diction, phrasing and dramatic interpretation that Streisand produced.

Streisand showed her anxiety only in the patter between songs. Charming, gossipy and a bit breathless, she plugged local sports teams, rhapsodized over the just-opened Gay Games and joked about being outclassed on the street by a flock of male Streisand impersonators. An autobiographical narrative, illustrated by family photos and film clips, wove through the concert, reminding us of how many people Streisand has been in real life as well as on-screen.

Conspicuously missing from the retrospective were men—the hapless ex-husband (Elliott Gould) or macho boy-toys (Ryan O'Neal, Jon Peters, Pierre Trudeau, Don Johnson, Andre Agassi). Streisand oohed and aahed over a spectral dream date—a few frames of young Marlon Brando in *Guys and Dolls*—but would brook no carnal male intruders into her divine female realm. Curiously, the token man was her son, Jason, whose progress from infancy to adulthood was charted in a blizzard of photos showing Streisand hovering like a vulture or posing with him like bride and groom. In the printed program, she sensuously nestles against his chest like his fiancée, who, if the tabloids are to be believed, is unlikely to materialize soon.

At the end of the show, like a climactic thunderburst of fireworks, we were treated to a dizzying *Citizen Kane*–like montage of liberal Democratic politics. As headlines flashed and photos whizzed by, the Berlin Wall fell, NAFTA passed and Hillary Rodham Clinton and Ruth Bader Ginsburg rose like titans. Look on the sunny side, Streisand counseled us, and stop sniping at our poor president. After this p.c. Nicene Creed we were blessed and sent back into the world to sin no more.

Thinking about the concert afterward, I recognized that "entertainment" is too impoverished a word for what superstars like Streisand do. As with the Romantic poets, her life and work are one; complaining about her ego is like spitting at a force of nature. Her materialism—the sharp deals, the acquisition of objects, the compulsive redecorating—is her ritualistic way of anchoring herself in externals, of rebalancing herself against the buffeting emotional vortex from which she draws her knowledge of the psyche. However one views her politics—which have been more consistent over the decades than most people realize—there is no way to deny her scintillating intelligence or her profound perception as an artist.

The Madison Square Garden concert was characteristically over-structured, so the audience's appetite for ovations was curbed and frustrated. This is Streisand's remarkable difference from Judy Garland, another gay-male idol whose signature song, "The Man That Got Away," she eerily performed. Garland was gluttonously naked before her audiences, with

223

whom she had marathon orgiastic energy exchanges. Streisand's coldness to her fans as individuals is self-protective. Of the century's sex goddesses, only Marlene Dietrich rivals Streisand in her cool, canny nurturing of health and husbanding of persona. Unlike Garland, Streisand has never self-destructed in booze and drugs, and unlike Madonna, she has never cheapened and overexposed herself by frivolous partying in nightclubs and locker rooms.

Diehard fans like me still love the early androgynous Streisand, with her campy humor and extreme drag-queen mannerisms. We suffered through her mundane, mop-headed period and rejoiced when she recovered her chic persona as the steely psychiatrist, all legs and nails, in *The Prince of Tides*. Her appearance and performance at President Clinton's inaugural gala were electrifying. She had literally grown into her nose: that bravely preserved ethnic badge now seemed like the prow of a ship cutting into the future. Perched at contrapposto angles on her stool, she looked, with her swinging arcs of honey-blonde hair, like the Winged Victory of Samothrace.

Those who dislike Streisand find her strident and overbearing, like Bea Arthur in *Maude*. Even Roseanne Arnold, no little chickadee, was daunted when they met, and accused Streisand of behaving like the "queen of the United States." But Streisand practically invented the modern concept of "bitch." In a 1992 speech she protested what she regarded as a sexist underestimation of her as a director: "A man is forceful—a woman is pushy . . . He's assertive—she's aggressive. He strategizes—she manipulates." But the power of the bitch is rooted in nature. Female sexuality, which Streisand freely uses on and off the set, is always destabilizing.

When she gets on her soapbox, Streisand can be a bore. Witness, for example, her affected endorsement of a 1992 boycott of the entire state of Colorado because of anti-gay Amendment 2. Didactic moods make Streisand lose all sense of humor, normally one of her greatest gifts. She has never realized the ancient stature of comedy as an art form. She was wonderful as a Jerry Lewis gamine in *What's Up, Doc?*, a film she detests as "infantile." Conversely, her efforts to be "serious" often sink her in tar pits of schlock. Historical context gets obliterated, as in *Yentl*, where a gritty re-creation of Eastern European Jewish village life flattens out into soap opera. Humorless Streisand ends up in bathos, as in *A Star Is Born*, a neglected film of unheralded virtues, which are murdered in the excruciating seven-minute coda, where we seem trapped with her emoting, decapitated head in a damp diving bell.

The importance of Streisand's deprived Brooklyn childhood—the rejecting mother, the dead father and the bleak, cramped quarters—has been overstated. These are diminishing psychodramas in our era of victimhood. Artists of Streisand's dimension have power and aggression on a massive scale virtually from birth. There will always be a clash between originality and environment, even under the best of circumstances. Streisand's singular imagination has filtered and processed three decades of our collective life. A unique combination of earthiness and elegance, sensitivity and assertion, she remains one of the great symbols of modern woman, independent, self-directed, always in process.

*A*ll of Barbra Streisand's LPs have been re-released on CD, except for *The Owl and the Pussycat*, and that's just dialogue anyway. But if you want to go deeper into Barbra collecting than just a shelf of records—and there are thousands around the world who do—here's a guide to some of the more popular collectibles and what they're likely to set you back.

TOP TEN MUSIC RARITIES
BARBRA STREISAND—THE EVENT OF THE DECADE/
A RETROSPECTIVE
March 1994/Columbia XPCD417/UK Promo
$350
Double CD/This is an astonishing 44-track CD set promoting Barbra's concerts in London. Includes 17 of Barbra's all-time greatest hits plus other popular songs. Plain packaging without any pictures. Back cover does list dates of London concerts. Very rare and expensive.

Barbra: Ordinary Miracles
June 1994/Columbia CSK 6120/Promo
$25–$40
CD Promo/This is a 19-track CD promo. Includes studio and live versions of Ordinary Miracles. Plus 17 tracks of Greatest Hits. Color insert is the same as commercial release. Backside of insert includes list of tour dates.

Barbra Streisand—Special Selections
1992/Sony/Japan XDDP 93080-1/Radio Demo
$350+
2 CD Set/Hits and selections from Just for the Record and The Prince of Tides. Special color booklet. Limited 100 pressing. Pricey.

All I Ask of You
CD Picture Disc/1988
CBS/UK Import/Picture Disc/4 Tracks
$75+

We're Not Making Love Anymore
CD Picture Disc/1989
CBS/UK Import/Picture Disc 3 Tracks
$75

Places That Belong to You
CD Picture Disc/1992
CBS/UK Import/Picture Disc 4 Tracks
$75

The Way He Makes Me Feel
LP Picture Disc (Promo only)
(film and studio versions—dbl.-sided picture disc)
$40–$60

Emotion Picture LP
$35–$50

The Legend of Barbra Streisand/1983
Columbia A25 1779
2 LP Radio Show/Greatest Hits and Yentl tracks, with interview
$50+

Barbra Streisand—Portrait of an Artist/1992
Westwood Productions
4 LP Radio Show/Commentary by Streisand. Broadcast on radio during February 1992. Limited pressing of 150 sets or less. Mix of Greatest Hits, Just for the Record and The Prince of Tides.
$200–$250

TOP 10X2 RARE NON-ALBUM 45RPM–7" SINGLES

(Bold items never appeared on an album. Most sell for $8 to $15. The foreign-issued "Evergreen" 45s sell for over $50–$75 each. The French EP sells for $75 and up.)

33078	**Happy Days Are Here Again/When the Sun Comes Out** (1962 Versions)
No Num.	**Lover Come Back to Me/My Coloring Book** (1962 Versions)
13-33078	**Happy Days Are Here Again/My Coloring Book** (Hall of Fame Reissue)
4-42965	People/**I Am Woman** (solo version)
4-43127	**Funny Girl**/Absent Minded Me (This Funny Girl version was never used for Broadway play.)
4-43248	**Why Did I Choose You?*/My Love**** (*Long version, **Alternate to My Pa)
CBS 6048	En Francais (4 Track EP/France only) **Les enfants Qui Pleurents** (Martina) & **Et La Mer** (Look), alternates from Je m'Appelle Barbra
4-44474	**Our Corner of the Night/He Could Show Me**
4-44622	**Funny Girl/I'd Rather Be Blue**
4-44704	My Man/**Don't Rain On My Parade**
4-44775	**Frank Mills**/Punky's Dilemma
4-45072	**Before the Parade Passes By**/Love Is Only Love
4-45147	**The Best Thing You've Ever Done**/Summer Me, Winter Me
AE-24 DJ	**On a Clear Day** (Stereo)/**On a Clear Day** (Mono) (Columbia versions)
4-45944	**The Way We Were***/What Are You Doing the Rest of Your Life (*Alternate of LP version)
3-10272	**Shake Me, Wake Me** (long and short versions)
CBS 5101	**Evergreen (Italian)**/Evergreen (English)
CBS 5866	**Evergreen (French)**/Evergreen (English)
10555	**Evergreen (Spanish)**/Evergreen (English)
38-04357	**Papa, Can You Hear Me?** (with string intro)

Stockpiling video footage is basic Barbra collecting. Pricing the "cost" is difficult at best, since it's not officially released material. Most of these shows have only been broadcast once. Most fans can "trade" or buy this video from other Barbra collectors, paying up to $30 for a mixed two-hour tape.

TOP RARE TELEVISION SPECIALS
(TV Specials broadcast only once.)

1973—Barbra Streisand & Other Musical Instruments (CBS Special)
1975—Funny Girl to Funny Lady (ABC Special)
1976—With One More Look At You (Syndicated)
1983—A Film Is Born—The Making of Yentl (Syndicated)
1995—Barbra—The Concert (CBS broadcast/additional material)

TOP TEN TELEVISION INTERVIEWS

1975—Today Show (2 parts)
1976—Barbara Walters Special
1983—Today Show (5 parts)
1983—20/20—Full hour profile
1985—Barbara Walters Special
1986—The Today Show (3 parts)
1991—60 Minutes
1991—Today Show (3 parts)
1991—Larry King Live (full hour)
1993—20/20

TOP SINGING APPEARANCES

1963—The Dinah Shore Special
1963—Jack Parr Show (11–29)
1963—The Bob Hope Special (9–27)
1963—Ed Sullivan Show (3–24)

1963—Ed Sullivan Show (6–9)
1971—Burt Bacharach Special (3–14)
1977—Academy Awards (3–28)
1978—The Stars Salute Israel (5–8)
1980—Grammy Awards (2–27)
1991—Earth Day Special

TOP 10 AWARD PRESENTATIONS/APPEARANCES

1965—Emmy Awards/Receives Emmy Award
1969—Academy Awards/Wins Best Actress
1970—Academy Awards/Presents Best Actor Award to John Wayne
1977—Academy Awards/Sings Evergreen and wins award
1984—Golden Globe Awards/Best Picture and Director awards
1986—Grammy Awards/Award to Mrs. Ira Gershwin
1986—Academy Awards/Best Director Award to Sidney Pollack
1992—Grammy Awards/Grammy Legend Award
1992—Saturday Night Live/Coffee Talk Skit
1992—Academy Awards

TOM'S TEN MOST COLLECTIBLE ALBUMS
(All are available as CDs. LPs are out-of-print.)

My Name Is Barbra, Two/Oct. 1965
Simply Streisand/Oct. 1967
Funny Girl Soundtrack/July 1968
Stoney End/Feb. 1971
Greatest Hits Vol. 2/Nov. 1978
Guilty/Sept. 1980
Yentl Soundtrack/Nov. 1983
The Broadway Album/Oct. 1985
Just for the Record/Sept. 1991
Back to Broadway/June 1993

TOP 10 MUSIC VIDEOS

My Heart Belongs to Me
You Don't Bring Me Flowers (commercial release)
Woman in Love (film clips only)
Memory (UK release only)
Left in the Dark
Emotion
Somewhere (commercial release)
We're Not Making Love Anymore
Places That Belong to You
For All We Know

TOP 10 MUSIC PROMOTION ITEMS

Barbra Joan Streisand Poster—Included in original album release
$3.50–$25
Live Concert at the Forum Poster—Included in original album release
$3.50–$25
Superman Standup—5 feet tall/Color
$75
Emotion Poster—36 × 36/Color
$25
The Broadway Album Poster—36 × 36/Color
$25
Back to Broadway Poster—24 × 36/BS standing with mike
$15
Back to Broadway Display—Large display of BS with mike
$75–$150
The Concert (CD/Video) Poster—24 × 36 full-color poster
$15
Display/Standup—Blockbuster display unit
$100–$150

CONCERT MERCHANDISE

Concert Program $25
Coffee Mug (Tour) $15
Cards $10
Watch $75
Black Picture T-shirt $25
White "Eyes" T-shirt $25
Tour Glass Paper Weight $60
Tote Bag $60
Post Cards $25
Color Poster $30
Black & White Poster $25

MOVIE MATERIAL

Yentl One Sheet $50
Funny Girl One Sheet/Academy Awards $150
The Prince of Tides Video Standup $75
The Prince of Tides Theater Standup $150+
Most Stills $4–$6 each
A Star Is Born Sundevil Stadium Poster $150+
The Prince of Tides Academy Award Promotion Program $50
Any Lobby Cards $5–$7 each
Any Film One Sheet $25+ (rolled or folded)
Film Programs $25–$50 each

PHOTO CREDITS

Photos on pp. xx and 146 courtesy of Archive Photos/Express Newspapers

Photos on pp. 20, 46, 65, 85, 192, 215, and 226 courtesy of Archive Photos

Photo on p. 100 courtesy of Archive Photos/Archive France

Photos on pp. 132, 163, 173, and 181 courtesy of Archive Photos/fotos international

COMING SOON IN HARDCOVER

Don't Block the Blessings

REVELATIONS OF A LIFETIME

PATTI LaBELLE

with Laura B. Randolph

 RIVERHEAD BOOKS